1970

This book may be kept

THE MUSIC OF
GUSTAV
HOLST

THE MUSIC OF
GUSTAV
HOLST

═══

IMOGEN HOLST

═══

SECOND EDITION

LONDON
OXFORD UNIVERSITY PRESS
NEW YORK   TORONTO
1968

Oxford University Press, Ely House, London W. 1

GLASGOW   NEW YORK   TORONTO   MELBOURNE   WELLINGTON
CAPE TOWN   SALISBURY   IBADAN   NAIROBI   LUSAKA   ADDIS ABABA
BOMBAY   CALCUTTA   MADRAS   KARACHI   LAHORE   DACCA
KUALA LUMPUR   HONG KONG   TOKYO

PRINTED LITHOGRAPHICALLY IN GREAT BRITAIN
AT THE UNIVERSITY PRESS, OXFORD
BY VIVIAN RIDLER
PRINTER TO THE UNIVERSITY

TO

BENJAMIN BRITTEN

CONTENTS

FACSIMILES

NOTE

THIS book was written in 1948–50. At that time very little of my father's music had been recorded, apart from *The Planets*, and short works such as the *St. Paul's Suite* and the ballet music from *The Perfect Fool*. His mature works, including *Egdon Heath*, the *Choral Fantasia*, and *Hammersmith* were seldom heard: they had not yet been recorded, and the manuscript full scores were only available on hire. Many of the choral works that have since been republished were then unobtainable. A book that described the works therefore had its uses.

In 1962 *The Music of Gustav Holst* became out of print, but soon afterwards there was an astonishing increase in the demand for performances and recordings of his less familiar works, and in 1967 the Oxford University Press asked me if they could bring out a photographic reproduction of the book as a second impression. I should have liked to have been able to refuse, because so many of my opinions have altered as a result of listening to English music that has been written during the last twenty years. Today there is little difficulty in following the enharmonic changes in my father's bitonal works, and the counterpoint in the *Fugal Concerto* sounds gracious rather than brittle. Those rapid, persistent parallel fourths in the *Perfect Fool* ballet, in *Jupiter* and in the Bacchanal from the *Choral Symphony* no longer sound blatant in the late nineteen-sixties: there is an ironic edge to their liveliness that now seems entirely appropriate. And in his early works those nineteenth-century romantic harmonies are no longer so disconcerting: there are only six bars in *Savitri* that still make me feel embarrassed.

During the last few years it has been encouraging to hear young musicians disagreeing with many of the things I have written in this book. 'You are *quite wrong*,' they tell me. They have been able to listen to the music without being harassed by any problems of style, because the phrases that stood out as old-fashioned in 1948 have been swallowed up and digested in the process that we call history. Is it therefore a mistake to allow the opinions of twenty years ago to be brought back into print? It would be much more satisfactory to start all over again, delving once more into the manuscript 'Early Horrors' and re-learning each printed score. But the Oxford University Press, who are the most patient of publishers, could not wait as long as that. They have convinced me that it is worth bringing out a revised edition because, so far, this is the only detailed chronological study of my father's music. And although in the following pages I have often stressed his technical weaknesses, I have always tried to hear them from his own point of view. After all, the weaknesses were only temporary setbacks that eventually helped to lead him on his journey towards his most mature works. The outline of that journey has not changed, and it is still true to say that he was struggling throughout most of his life. That struggle is what this book is about.

I wish to thank the publishers mentioned on page 158 for their permission to quote extracts from my father's works. The facsimile facing page 126 is reproduced by permission of Boosey & Hawkes, Ltd. My thanks are also due to the Clarendon Press for allowing me to quote from the works of Robert Bridges; to Victor Gollancz and Miss Ann Wolfe for lines from Humbert Wolfe's poems, and to Messrs. Constable & Co., Ltd. for extracts from the late Helen Waddell's translations of medieval latin lyrics.

Several factual details in the text that are no longer accurate have been corrected, and the list of compositions has been brought up to date where works have been reprinted by a different publisher. The lecture on 'The Teaching of Art' has been included as an appendix: it is taken from *Heirs and Rebels* (O.U.P. 1959) which is now out of print.

Where a chord is mentioned in the text, C represents 'middle' C, C^1 an octave above it, and C_1 an octave below it. (I should have liked to modernize this system, but as this edition is a photographic reproduction it would have involved too many changes.)

I. H.

Aldeburgh
January 1968

CHAPTER I

BACKGROUND TO THE 'EARLY HORRORS'
(1893–1900)

WHEN Holst died in 1934 much of his music was still unfamiliar. Many audiences knew *The Planets* and *The Hymn of Jesus*, and many amateur choirs and orchestras knew the short works he had written for them to sing and play. But his early compositions were only remembered by the few enthusiasts who had taken part in the first performances, and his later works were only understood by the few explorers who were undaunted by the austerity of his counterpoint.

During the years since his death, this aloof austerity in the later works has become easier to accept, while the painful blunders in the early works have become easier to forgive. At the time when this book was written, in 1948, much of his music was still unfamiliar. Since then, some of his best works, such as *Egdon Heath*, the *Choral Fantasia*, and the *Lyric Movement* have been recorded. But many full scores are still in manuscript, and it seems unlikely that some of the out-of-print piano scores will ever reappear, for they belong to that vast lumber-room where much of the English music written during the first quarter of this century has found a fit resting-place.

It is a depressing occupation to go through the entire collection of Holst's early failures, but it helps to solve the problem of why some of the greatest of his music is uneven and incomplete. Studying the works chronologically, it is possible to recognize the same strength and the same weaknesses recurring throughout his creative life.

But it is not yet possible to see him in a clear perspective: the difficulties he had to overcome are still too recent to be considered dispassionately. Nor is it easy to escape getting entangled in frequent changes of fashion. A few years ago his early part-songs from *The Princess* seemed hopelessly old-fashioned; today they are sung with unabashed delight. But his neo-modal works of the nineteen-twenties sound spineless today, and are shunned by many of the singers and players who once greeted them with rapture. The *Terzetto* in three keys baffled several distinguished musicians who heard it when it was first tried through in 1925. Even Holst himself was not quite sure whether it was real music or not; he had to listen to it several times before he could make up his mind about it. In 1945 it was warmly welcomed by listeners in the depths of the country who had not yet been faced with the necessity of learning their key-signatures.

There are moments in some of his works that immediately sound familiar at a first hearing: the mind goes out to meet them, for their mood and inflection belong to the music of the nineteen-sixties. It is difficult not to get over-excited at this contemporary quality in his music, but it is still more difficult to avoid getting impatient when he falls short of his own greatness, as in the weak patches that destroy the unity of *The Hymn of Jesus*. He was defeated by these weaknesses over and over again, and it was not until the very end of his life that he began to reach the security of freedom, after the long and severe struggles of a journey which had lasted over forty years.

It was in May 1893 that he came to London to study composition under Stanford at the Royal College of Music. London was bewilder-ingly full of opportunities for making fresh discoveries about music: Tchaikovsky was conducting his latest symphony at a Philharmonic concert; the Brahms clarinet quintet had been a recent novelty at the St. James's Hall; Wagner enthusiasts were still talking about last year's Ring at Covent Garden under Mahler—it was only the second time the work had been heard in England. Ebenezer Prout had just finished writing his book on 'Musical Form', and Arnold Dolmetsch was lecturing on the lute to members of the Incorporated Society of Musicians. Travellers from Europe were discussing the first per-formance of Verdi's new opera 'Falstaff', and there were rumours that Debussy was writing a most astonishing string quartet.

Coming up from Gloucestershire, the 18-year-old Holst brought with him a lively imagination, a sense of humour, an adequate piano technique, some useful experience as a village organist and choir-master, and the manuscript of an operetta called *Lansdown Castle* which had recently been performed at the Corn Exchange, Chelten-ham. He also brought with him the inestimable blessing of having been born into a family in which his father, his grandfather, and his great-grandfather had all been hard-working professional musicians. Ever since he could remember there had been music going on all day, every day: rehearsals for his father's orchestral concerts at the Rotunda, choral practices at All Saints' Church, and an endless string of piano pupils playing Mendelssohn in the front room. He himself had been practising Liszt and Chopin for four or five hours a day until neuritis had compelled him to give up all thoughts of being a concert pianist. His favourite modern composer was Grieg, but he had had to wait until his father was out of the house before playing the Lyric Pieces. However, he was able to share his father's enthusiasm for the operas of Gilbert and Sullivan—each new vocal score was explored from beginning to end, with eager and serious thoroughness.

His own earliest composition was a setting of the poem *Horatius* for chorus and orchestra. A note in the margin of that spidery but determined-looking full score says: 'This was written before I knew any harmony or counterpoint, probably in 1887. The only book on the theory of music that I knew was Berlioz's Instrumentation which I knew practically by heart. I wrote this in secret bit by bit until one day—the family being out—I tried to play it on the piano. The result was that I never wrote another note of it.' His next attempts at composition were not much more successful, but he found things easier in 1892, after he had spent four months in Oxford studying strict counterpoint.

Traces of the counterpoint lessons can be heard in the operetta *Lansdown Castle*: at one point in the score, a four-part fugue of deliberate orthodoxy is made to serve as a chorus of ironical laughter, each minim or crotchet being sung to the syllable 'Ha!' The work is full of pleasing tunes, faultlessly made to the Sullivan pattern, and his experience as conductor of a Cotswold Choral Society had taught him to string the tunes together with the least possible fuss, so that the joins could be managed by every would-be passenger in the back row of the chorus. It is characteristic of him that even at this early stage in his career he should be meticulously careful about details of cueing-in: he gives the heroine a cadenza soaring up to top C, but he takes the precaution of adding an alternative version in brackets going no higher than G. Unfortunately the Cheltenham audience of 1893 was shocked by the one really dramatic moment in the work, where he uses a fragment of an Anglican chant as a magic incantation, asking his chorus to sing it through closed lips, *molto crescendo*, in unaccompanied consecutive fifths.

Lansdown Castle was something of an achievement: he had to wait more than twenty years before his next operatic production. But the excitement of hearing it sung and seeing it acted on a real stage was soon swept aside by the most overwhelming experience of his eighteen years of life, when he listened to Bach's B minor Mass at the Three Choirs Festival in Worcester Cathedral.

It was a revelation that lasted for a lifetime. The music penetrated far beyond the familiar sounds that were already lodged in the surface of his memory. From then onwards several threads of Bach's thought may have lain waiting until the time when he could weave them into the fabric of his own musical experience: perhaps his listening mind made room to receive the desolation of that falling diminished third in the second Kyrie, the tranquillity of those rising sixths over the held pedal in 'et in terra pax', the conviction of the plainsong Credo with its procession of crotchets moving down-hill in the bass, the cheerful drop of a major seventh at 'Patrem omnipotentem', the dazzling intensity of the tenors' C natural against the chord of E major in the Crucifixus, and the piling up of the melodic fourths in 'et expecto'. Holst never spoke of these moments or of the possible influence they may have had on his own music, though he mentioned his exaltation at first hearing the Sanctus, and he has described the physical effect that it had on him: how he felt as if he were floating far above the heads of the other listeners in the cathedral, and how he found himself clutching the sides of his chair to prevent himself from bumping his head against the roof. But there were no words with which he could describe the effect that it had on his mind and spirit.

Not that it made any immediate difference to his compositions. He continued to turn out songs that were mock Sullivan and piano pieces that were imitation Grieg. Years afterwards he collected all the manuscripts he had written while he was having lessons from Stanford and tied them up in a brown paper parcel labelled 'Early Horrors'. Very few of them show any signs of the individual mind that was one day to emerge, though it is possible to recognize his delight in the texture of eight-part counterpoint for unaccompanied female voices, as well as his fondness for ostinato bare fifths in five-four.

His Opus I, a comic opera called *The Revoke*, is not much of an improvement on *Lansdown Castle*; relying on its Sullivanesque tunes, it tries desperately hard to be witty except in the moments when it succeeds in being sentimental. But the orchestration shows a sense of adventure and there is an occasional turn of phrase that is unmistakably his own:

Ex. 1.

These three rising quavers, with their change of stress at each repetition and their rush into diminution as they approach an unexpected chord, are a genuine landmark in the midst of their borrowed surroundings.

Another one-act opera, *The Magic Mirror*, which was discarded long before it was finished, has a rough sketch of a fugue for strings with characteristic rising melodic fourths and a clash of E♯ against E♮:

Ex. 2.

But in the revised version the tune has been fattened up with thick slices of chords, the time signature has been changed to three-four, the rising fourths have become portentously dotted sequences, the *Andante quasi adagio* has given way to *Moderato ma Agitato* and a stage direction tells us that the hero is 'discovered reading in the red glow of sunset which gradually deepens'. For Holst, by now, was helpless in the throes of Wagner-worship. Tristan had transformed his whole existence and for the next ten years he was held by the binding tyranny of its spell. This was an influence that had far more immediate and spectacular results than the revelation of the B minor Mass. Bach's music had sunk to the very depths of his being, and lay there, biding its time. Wagner's music was continually with him, swirling round and round in his brain and shuddering through every nerve of his body. He not only dreamed Wagner, he moved Wagner, he ate and drank Wagner and took in huge draughts of Wagner with every gasp of air he breathed along the Prince Consort Road. By an effort he managed to shut most of it out of his mind when he was employed in writing school songs for small children: fortunately his practical experience prompted him that it would be safer to stick to

B

Sullivan. But in his orchestral works he let his passion have its way with him: every change of harmony had to be chromatic, every motif had to be dealt with in sequence. Even if he had been powerful enough to prevent it, he would have been unwilling to interfere with the persistent way in which a secondary seventh lurked round every emotional corner.

Stanford's lessons had a sobering effect: week after week his part-songs and instrumental exercises were greeted with the familiar verdict: 'It won't do, me boy, it won't do.' By the time Holst left the Royal College of Music he had learned to be his own critic in matters of craftsmanship, and could turn out competent pieces of chamber-music and pleasant-sounding works for chorus and orchestra. But he had an immense distance to travel before he could find the right musical language for what he wanted to say.

The 'Early Horrors' make doleful reading. The sentimental songs for solo voice and piano occasionally betray the need for a brief respite from chromaticism, but they show very little feeling for the rhythm of the words. There are rare gleams of genuine imagination, but they are soon smothered under the weight of all those secondary sevenths. Without realizing it, he was already trying to free himself from the overpowering influence of Wagner's music. Signs of the struggle can be heard in the orchestral *Winter Idyll* where the wintriness is of a Scandinavian variety, borrowed from Grieg: Holst's own Scandinavian ancestors were cut off from him by too great a distance in years to allow any lingering recollections of that frozen darkness. It is a fairly convincing winter of its kind, though the naïve melodies give the impression that they are sitting about a little uncomfortably in their heroic armour. An unaccompanied cor anglais solo has a melancholy of its own that is feeling its way towards the *Somerset Rhapsody*, and there is a glimpse of a later Holst in the ostinato cross-rhythms of the strings. A sudden outbreak of descending minor ninths, slurred over the bar-line and punctuated with dramatic rests, might seem at first glance to be an early example of what was long afterwards to become a favourite interval, but at second glance they turn out to be no more than ponderous fragments of an extended chromatic scale, irrevocably mixed up with the harmonies that engulf them and quite unable to stand on their own legs as melodic intervals.

There are no signs of any struggle to escape from secondary sevenths in *Ornulf's Drapa*, a scena for baritone and orchestra. A blanket of impenetrable gloom hangs over the work. At times the declamation is perilously like the Wagnerian parody in *The Perfect Fool*: perhaps

the words are responsible, for it is difficult to do less than full justice
to such lines as 'sorrow-laden singer, singing, suffers surely', or
'Song-craft's glorious god-gift stauncheth woe and wailing'. But in
1898, when Holst was steeping himself in the writings of Ibsen, no
breath of frivolous questioning could stir the heavy atmosphere of its
solemnity.

In both the *Winter Idyll* and *Ornulf's Drapa* there is a sure touch in
the orchestration. By now he had had several years' experience as a
trombone player and he was getting an inside knowledge of what an
orchestra could do. It was fortunate for him that he had had to supple-
ment his composition scholarship by playing trombone in theatre
orchestras: it taught him far more than he would ever have got out
of a text-book, and it was one of the most important things that
happened to him during his four and a half years of training at the
college. Stanford's lessons in craftsmanship also had a lasting effect
on the clarity of his writing: it was Stanford who had taught him to
refuse to rely on cast-iron rules, and who had insisted that he must
learn his technique so completely that he could afford to forget it.
Most important of all was his close friendship with Vaughan Williams, a
friendship that continued throughout his life. It was Vaughan Williams
who opened doors leading to other worlds of thought; Holst borrowed
books from him, and learnt that there were many ways of searching
for truth and beauty. Listening to William Morris, he realized that
'art must be part of the daily life of every man, to be shared by learned
and unlearned, as a language that all can understand'. Reading Walt
Whitman's poetry, he groped his way towards a feeling of unity with
all men and all life. On his solitary walks along the towing-path at
Hammersmith he would remember:

The impalpable sustenance of me from all things at all hours of the day,
The simple, compact, well-join'd scheme, myself disintegrated, everyone
    disintegrated yet part of the scheme,
The similitudes of the past and those of the future,
The glories strung like beads on my smallest sights and hearings, on the
    walk in the street and the passage over the river.

The overture, *Walt Whitman*, written in 1899, was an attempt to
convey what Whitman's poetry had meant to him, but his intentions
were wrecked by wallowing. It is a thick and brassy work, its voluptu-
ous chords moving chromatically outwards with *marcato* deliberation.

During that same year he wrote the *Suite de Ballet*, a work that one
can hardly listen to without flinching at the banality of its borrowed
romanticism. The 'Danse Rustique' inevitably conjures up visions of

a nineteenth-century operatic 'entry of peasants': he had got to wait another six years before hearing the folk-tunes that would have saved him from such inadequate writing. The Valse is even worse: the solidly built tune does its level best to get around as well as it can, but is held earth-bound by its flat-footed crotchets. A 'Scene de Nuit' meanders through pages and pages of stickily monotonous twelve-eight, and it is not until the 'Carnival' that the genuine Holst appears for a few brief moments, as in the opening staccato leap:

Ex. 3.

His biggest work at this time was the *Cotswolds Symphony*. It was meant to express his deep love of the Cotswold hills, but his feelings are scarcely recognizable. Searching for a symbol of the English country-side he found nothing to build on except the imitation Tudor heartiness of Edward German. It was a makeshift symbol, and having borrowed it, he hardly knew what to do with it, beyond placing it in the approved mould, and hoping it would turn out all right. The first movement makes all the correct gestures and travels in the appropriate directions but it bears no resemblance to the journey of his mind while walking the stretch of hills between Wyck Rissington and Bourton-on-the-Water. The slow movement, an Elegy in memory of William Morris, has moments in it where the intensity of his thought breaks through the inadequacies of his language. (See Facsimile.) Here the words 'senza espress' make their first appearance, showing the beginnings of a line of thought that was to lead him through the 'dead' *pp* of *Neptune* to the mysterious monotony of *Egdon Heath*.

It is by far the best movement in the work. There is nothing characteristic about the Scherzo except the fact that its tune is built on a structure of melodic fourths, while in the last movement he is back once again in a surge of chromatic modulations and striving sequences. There was to be no escape from their clutches for many years to come.

SLOW MOVEMENT OF THE *COTSWOLDS SYMPHONY*

CHAPTER II

CHROMATICISM AND THE MYSTIC TRUMPETER

(1900–5)

HIS apprenticeship was long and painful. While working at the *Cotswolds Symphony* he continued to turn out part-songs that had little to distinguish them from the exercises he had taken to his lessons every week when he was still a student at college. His four-part settings of poems by William Morris and Francis Thompson are competent but uneventful, with nothing to recommend them beyond the singableness one would expect from any of Stanford's intelligent ex-pupils. Occasionally there is a welcome lightness in the texture— he had been copying out several Morley balletts for his socialist choir in Hammersmith, and he was discovering that there were English words which needed to be sung trippingly on the tongue.

He was happiest when writing for unaccompanied female voices; perhaps the limitations of their compass forced him into the economy that was one day to prove his salvation. The eight-part *Ave Maria* is the first of the early compositions that sounds convincing when performed today. It is not just a matter of 'good' counterpoint, with every entry carefully prepared, and every line equally interesting to sing; the work has also got the rare and unaccountable quality that transforms each member of an amateur chorus into a much better singer than usual. Several phrases suggest a later Holst: the piling up of the seconds and fourths as they rise from a unison, and the smooth transition from one unadorned triad to another, as if in anticipation of the influence that Tudor church music was to have on his writing. Throughout the *Ave Maria* there is a richness in the close-knit diatonic passing-notes that is very much nearer to his mature use of discords than the welter of added chromaticisms in his early orchestral works. And in the choice of six-four, he is instinctively turning away from the ponderously pious utterances of the Victorian church music he had known in Cheltenham and is moving towards the freedom of *This have I done for my true love*.

After the serenity of the *Ave Maria* it is depressing to come upon the one-act opera called *The Youth's Choice*, a work he afterwards withdrew from his list of compositions. It was his first serious opera, and it was damned from the outset by its impossible libretto. He had insisted on writing it himself, in spite of several warnings from Vaughan Williams, who had advised him to read Malory and to keep off picturesque words that had lost their meaning. But Holst was obstinate about it. And being immersed in Tristan and the Ring, he was powerless to prevent the libretto from distorting itself into the idiom of a translation from Wagner. When the Father (bass), first meets the Knight (tenor), he exclaims: 'Truly I see thou art strong, brave, and handsome, Fit mate for my child.' Such disasters are liable to occur on any page of the score, heavily underlined with the chord C♯E G B.

Holst's experience as repetiteur for the Carl Rosa Opera Company had not given him much sense of the stage. The characters in *The Youth's Choice* hang around aimlessly, hoping to make their meaning a little clearer by repeating what they have just said at a different level of pitch. The false timing is exasperating to the point of absurdity. When the Elder Sister rushes on to the stage, breathless with excitement, announcing that the Knight has been victorious at the jousts and is at that very instant speeding on his way to claim her as his bride, the heavy Father chooses this most inopportune of all moments to plant himself firmly in the middle of the stage. Turning to his two daughters, he asks: 'Will ye list to a story?' 'Yea, Father', says the obedient Elder Sister. 'Right gladly', replies the Younger. He thereupon recites a legend out of a book. It is a *very* long story, and, while he is taking his time over it, the stage directions inform us that the inevitable 'red glow of the sunset gradually deepens'.

There is one significant indication of the way Holst's mind was working: as the singer quotes the legend of the lamp which the youth holds in his hand to illumine his life, wood-wind and tremolo strings play the chord F₁B₁E A♭ for the word 'gaze'. Although the clash is immediately resolved in a conventional nineteenth-century fashion, for one instant we are given a glimpse of the dazzling light of 'To you who gaze a lamp am I'. (Ex. 37.)

The Youth's Choice would make an excellent parody of Wagner-worship if it were produced today exactly as it stands. But there is something of Holst's single-minded sincerity in the work. It shows through the cracks in the structure, so that the climax of renunciation is moving in spite of its absurd embellishments.

It was his single-minded sincerity that had led him to explore the philosophy of the Bhagavad Gîtâ. The idea of non-attachment was to have a lasting influence on his life and on his music. Since 1899 he had been trying to learn Sanskrit, and had been working laboriously at his own translations of hymns from the Rig Veda and dramatic episodes from the Ramayana. The symphonic poem *Indra* was the first thing he wrote as a direct result of his studies of Sanskrit literature, but there is very little trace of a newly discovered world of thought in this particular manifestation of the god of rain and storm. The large orchestra rushes up and down hill in turbulant chromatic sixths and plunges into prolonged climaxes round the chord of the diminished seventh, or breaks into cascades of wood-wind arpeggios against high divisi tremolo strings, without any essential fervour in the music to justify all the noise. But there are occasional hints of the mood of the *Rig Veda* in the quiet sixths for oboes:

Ex. 4.

and in the fragment of a tune for cellos:

Ex. 5.

Invocation to Dawn, for baritone and piano, is the earliest of his settings of Sanskrit hymns from the *Rig Veda*. It shows that the out-line of the version he wrote five years later was already in his mind, but here the words limp unhappily in their three-four harness, and the piano accompaniment, with its non-stop quaver arpeggios, might be a Chopin prelude with the tune left out.

There is little to redeem the banality of the other solo songs belong-ing to this period: in his settings of Elizabethan lyrics he is content to pile up the chromatic modulations while throbbing from one platitude to the next. It is difficult to realize that he had not yet heard a lutenist song. Nearly all the riches of the sixteenth-century madrigals and motets were still locked up beyond his reach. Ten years later, when the first volumes of Fellowes's edition of the English madrigal composers began to appear, he became so steeped in his love of the Elizabethans that, as he himself said, he was 'never quite the same man' afterwards. But in 1903 he knew only the half-dozen rounds and madrigals which he had copied from the British Museum, and in his own settings of the lyrics he seldom avoided distorting the words out of all recognition. He was far less stilted with Tennyson, allowing the 'silvery gossamers that twinkle into green and gold' to lead him into his earliest attempt at a *quasi recitative*.

While exploring the possibilities of contemporary English poetry he had already discovered his close sympathy with the work of both Bridges and Hardy, two writers who were afterwards to become his friends. But his setting of Bridges' *I will not let thee go* is separated by more than twenty years from the grace and ease of *Love on my heart from heaven fell*, and it is a shock to find what an immeasurable distance lies between them in thought and feeling. Nor is it easy, while writhing under the bathos of his setting of Hardy's *In a wood*, to remember that this same struggling mind would one day stretch to the greatness of *Egdon Heath*.

The inadequacy of these early solos haunted him long afterwards, when he was filled with distress to be reminded of the sickly sentimentality he had since learned to shun as 'the supreme crime in art'.

The liveliest of the early songs are those that were specially written for children. He had been teaching for several years at a small school in Barnes, and he knew what was wanted when writing for children's voices. *The Idea*, an operetta designed for his pupils, is imitation Sullivan from beginning to end, but it shows far better stage sense than *The Youth's Choice*, for the timing had to be arranged so that the children could go on acting while they were singing. And his practical experience as a conductor in choral societies helped to save him from several pitfalls in the writing of *King Estmere*, a ballad for chorus and orchestra in which the music has a character of its own that is never totally submerged in the flood of its chromatic sequences. There is a sense of continuity about it, and flashes of dramatic contrast, as well as an exciting moment when his own voice can be heard in a trumpet-tune over a ground bass.

Hardly a note of his own voice is recognizable in *A Song of the Night*, for violin solo and orchestra, but the opening rhapsodic cadenza, with its rising melodic fourths and its descending scale in sixths, has in it the germ of an idea that was to flower at the very end of his life in the *Lyric Movement*. A merciful silence should be kept

concerning some other pieces for violin which were afterwards with-
drawn from circulation: it is to be hoped they were written as pot-
boilers, since they coincide with the unhappy months when he was
trying to earn his living from his compositions.

At this time he was concentrating all his genuine thought and
energy on *The Mystic Trumpeter*, a setting of the poem by Walt
Whitman, for soprano solo and orchestra. It was the most important
work he had yet written, and it was his nearest approach to an expression of what he wanted to say. But it was doomed to failure, in spite
of its obvious strength and sincerity. For he had not yet found out
that Wagner's music marked the end of an epoch instead of the
beginning of a new golden age. He knew something was wrong
somewhere, but he was unable to realize that the wealth of harmonic
possibilities in Tristan had already been exhausted. Through the
disguise of the borrowed idiom he had clung to for so many years his
thought leaps out with startling directness:

Ex. 6.

This piercing pursuit was to follow him throughout the whole of his
life. Ten years later it breaks out into the terror of *Mars*. In another
fifteen years it challenges man's endurance in *Egdon Heath* and the
Choral Fantasia.

Several passages in *The Mystic Trumpeter* show that he was already
beginning to escape from applied chromaticism: 'the fretting world,
the streets, the noisy hours of day withdraw' is in the language of
Venus, and the tranquillity of 'Floating and basking upon heaven's
lake' foreshadows the *Ode to Death*.

The trouble begins when he tries to write ecstatically about love.
'Love that is all the earth to lovers' is unconvincing in its forced
ardour, while 'love that is crimson, sumptuous, sick with perfume'
grows more and more unreal from one note to the next. It is not only
the fulsome harmonies that sound false; it is also the clumsily
stereotyped declamation which interferes with any natural unfolding

of the rhythm of the words. He was soon to become aware of this, and it is interesting to compare the original version of one of the lines in *The Mystic Trumpeter* with the revised version he wrote several years later:

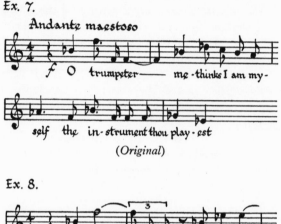

Ex. 7.

Andante maestoso

f O trumpeter—— me -thinks I am my-

self the in-strument thou play-est

(*Original*)

Ex. 8.

O trum - - pe-ter methinks I —

— am myself the in-strument thou playest

(*Revision of 1910*)

The revised version is only a patchwork affair, having been made to fit the existing orchestral accompaniment, but it shows that he was beginning to listen to the rhythm of the words and to allow his music to follow the instinctive rise and fall of each sentence.

Many years afterwards, he wrote to a friend, saying:

I find that *unconsciously* I have been drawn for years towards discovering the (or *a*) musical idiom of the English language. Never having managed to learn a foreign language, songs had always meant to me a peg of words on which to hang a tune. The great awakening came on hearing the recitatives in Purcell's Dido and Aeneas. Can you or anyone tell me how he managed *straight away* to write the only really musical idiom of the English language we have yet had?

Holst came very near to finding what he was searching for in the five songs for unaccompanied female voices from Tennyson's 'The

Princess'. In *O Swallow, Swallow* the words and the music are inseparable; the inflection of the opening phrase is caught up with the swoop and whirr of the swallow's flight through the air:

Ex. 9.

These were the last songs he wrote before the sudden impact of English folk-tunes changed the whole course of his musical life.

CHAPTER III

THE FOLK-SONG REVIVAL

(1905–7)

VAUGHAN WILLIAMS had begun collecting folk-songs in Essex during 1904, and as soon as Holst heard the tunes he recognized that this was what he had been longing for. Here, for the first time, he found the simplicity and economy that he needed in his own music. These short tunes seemed to contain within themselves the whole of what he wanted to say. Miraculously, they managed to combine an emotional beauty with an impersonal restraint. They were the living embodiment of the musical idiom of the English language, for the words and the music had grown up together and depended on each other for their very existence. He discovered that a flowing five-four could be the most natural and inevitable rhythm for the setting of an English poem. He also began to discover that music need not belong to a fixed major or minor key. He had been brought up to believe that a clearly established key was one of the first essentials in music, yet here was music that had never known a dominant seventh or its resolution. Holst never theorized about anything, and it is unlikely that he analysed any of the possibilities that lay hidden in this newly discovered region of sound. He was content to steep himself in the beauty of the songs until he had made that beauty a part of his own life.

It was not easy to shake off the old way of thinking and feeling. By an effort of the will he managed to persuade his nineteenth-century harmonies to shed layer after layer of protective chromaticism until they were left standing on the chill and unfamiliar brink of a Phrygian austerity.

The first painful stages of this process can be heard in the introduction to a setting of *Darest thou now, O soul*, written in 1905 and rejected soon afterwards:

Ex. 10.

Not that there is much to be said in favour of these chords: they might have had more vitality if he had left them the sprinkling of accidentals for which they still seem to crave. But they mark the first deliberate attempt to break away from the habits of the past ten years.

The two sets of folk-song accompaniments written in 1906 show some of the difficulties he had to overcome. One of the worst pitfalls was the apparent mixture of modes in some of the tunes: it often led him astray into thinking he ought to modulate. He had not been long enough acquainted with folk-songs to discover that both the flattened and the sharpened seventh can exist side by side without getting in each other's way.

But in spite of the unfamiliar idiom he was beginning to realize that these short tunes held within them their own harmonic possibilities. The accompaniment of 'I love my love' grows out of the shape of its Dorian tune:

Ex. 11.

He has arrived here at the very same chord that has been lying waiting for him at every climax throughout the long years of Wagner-worship. But when he is led to it by the unfolding of the harmonies within the mode's limitations this chord takes on such a different flavour that it is scarcely recognizable. He was not always so successful in the way he used it: having re-tasted its joys he was sometimes tempted to pick it out of its context and make a dramatic gesture with it, thereby transforming it into a small slice of imitation Brahms. Another temptation was to try and 'put in the expression' in the accompaniment. In his so-called 'free' arrangement of 'The Willow Tree', as soon as he loses sight of the narrow path of simplicity and economy, he gets hopelessly lost in the twilight and slithers about in a squelchy morass.

There was also the temptation of going to the opposite extreme and writing nothing but bare fifths and flattened sevenths:

Ex. 12.

This was perhaps the worst danger that threatened him in his new-found love. It was so easy to drift aimlessly on a sea of impotent tranquillity, without having to worry about any of the conflicts of tension or of stress. But fortunately these soothing sounds were too vague to ensnare him for very long. His temporary dose of barren purity served as a medicine in 1906, and as such it had its uses.

His first experiment in the extended use of folk-songs was an orchestral work called *Songs of the West*. It was a distressing failure. He had no idea how to deal with his tunes when they came one after another: at each change of key his obvious intentions stick out with the painfully exaggerated gesture of a nervous driver's traffic signs on the road. He knew that sonata form was no use to him here: the tunes were highly developed and complete in themselves, and he could hardly be expected to chop them up into small fragments just for the sake of putting them together again. So he set out to try to write in a form that would grow out of the songs. These early attempts at combining contrasted folk-tunes are clumsy and unconvincing: the bits of augmentation and canon sound laboured, and the sudden changes of speed are unsettling. He is more successful in the un-pretentious *Seven Scottish Airs* for strings and piano, where he makes little attempt to link the tunes but just goes straight on from one to another.

It is the development section that is the weakest part of the *Country Song*, the first of *Two Songs without Words* for small orchestra. His original tune for unaccompanied clarinet shows the effect of the new economy, but as soon as he attempts a bridge passage we hear the familiar quotations from Wagner: this time it is the Wagner of the Siegfried Idyll.

There is more of the undisguised Holst in the *Marching Song*; the sombre vitality of the opening brings the music near to the mood he shares with Hardy, and his second tune manages to sound noble without distending itself to the rank of *nobilmente*. Only one passage is unsatisfactory, where the modulating sequences are over-deliberate, and the melodrama sounds as if it has been stuck on to the surface of the music.

The *Somerset Rhapsody* for orchestra, founded on folk-songs, is also a mixture of good and bad writing. After the extreme simplicity of the opening, where the oboe plays the Sheep-Shearing Song under a held octave on muted violins, it is something of a shock to find him putting in the expression again, and reverting to the chromatic passing-notes of 'The Willow Tree':

Ex. 13.

In the first two bars he finds all the expression he needs within the limitations of the Dorian, but in the third bar he deliberately manufactures a nostalgic atmosphere. It is not just a question of which sort of harmony one prefers: the thing that matters is that it was essential for Holst to discover the emotional possibilities in the first two bars and to reject the trimmings in the third, for the whole of his art depended on extracting every particle of thought and feeling from the fewest notes. The bridge passages show that he was not going to be content with moving straight from one tune to the next and then labelling the work a Rhapsody. But some of these links are clumsy, in spite of the help of a ground bass. The weak patches seem obvious to us today, but in 1907 Holst was not able to put his finger on the tenth bar after 8 and ask himself, 'Is it necessary?' Because of these weaknesses the work as a whole sounds unsatisfactory, though it has moments of great beauty. It ends on a question mark. Up till now he had always taken it for granted that one should come home to rest on the tonic chord in its root position: it had been one of the unalterable laws. But that was now being swept aside, along with a good many other things.

The influence of folk-song helped him in his *Four Old English*

Carols for mixed voices and piano, where the directness of the medieval lyrics called forth an answering directness in his music and carried him a long way towards the 'tender austerity' that was to become his ideal. He was no scholar, and he knew nothing of the historical background to the words, but in *A babe is born* he instinctively ignored the artificial barriers between sacred and secular, linking the six-eight dance of the verse with the spacious liturgical harmonies of the unaccompanied Latin chorus. It is a return to a lost tradition that was later to flourish in the Whitsun festivals at Thaxted. In *Now let us sing* the sopranos' chiming descant in pianissimo staccato quavers must have been like a breath of fresh air to some of the carol singers of 1907. There is an influence of plainsong and of the polyphonic music of the sixteenth century in *Jesu, Thou the Virgin-Born*: he had been copying out motets by Victoria and di Lasso for his singing-classes at St. Paul's Girls' School, and he had found the serenity of their counterpoint unforgettable.

There is a rare beauty in these *Four Carols*, a beauty he was not always able to keep unspoiled during the next few years. For the struggle was not nearly over: it was only just beginning. The language of folk-tunes was a guide to him, but it was not his own language, and he could only apply its lesson if the mood and texture of his music demanded the utmost economy.

CHAPTER IV

THE SANSKRIT WORKS

(1906–12)

By the year 1906 he had finished *Sita*, the three-act opera he had begun working on as long ago as 1899. Most of it had been written before he had heard his first English folk-song, and it would have been impossible to try to alter it in the light of his new way of thinking. It would have meant scrapping it altogether, and he was not nearly ready to do that.

The libretto is his own adaptation of a Sanskrit story from the Ramayana. It sounds incurably like Wagner done into English, the prevailing mood being the heroic exaggeration of 'Now within my breast Hope burneth fiercely'. We are back again in the indispensable red glow of the sunset. Scenic effects and stage directions have a grandiose disregard for the practical difficulties of the producer. The action takes place in the ravine of a jungle or on the banks of a raging torrent into which the villain is hurled in the last scene. There are several furious battles: victims are killed and wounded: gods appear on a distant mountainside, lit by the shining moon or by the pearly light of dawn: hordes of devils enter, bearing flaming torches: a chariot with winged horses appears and mounts into the air during a flash of lightning. Everything is planned on a suitably colossal scale. The long-enduring soloists have to compete with an enormous orchestra in their efforts to provide the volume of tone demanded by the composer. When the heroine appears and catches a first glimpse of the man who is destined to be her husband, she flings back her shoulders and greets him by name on a high-held fortissimo A over a tremolo crescendo from the full orchestra.

'Good old Wagnerian bawling' was how Holst afterwards described *Sita*. But in spite of all its extravagance it is possible to recognize his own music striving to be heard: in a seven-four tune in a Phrygian scale with a sharpened sixth, in the dramatic repetition of the distant hammering of the bridge-builders, which is one of the few moments in the whole opera that shows any real grasp of the possibilities of writing for the stage, and in the struggle between the forces of good and evil, when the piercing pursuit of *The Mystic Trumpeter* grows more and more insistent at each answering challenge:

Ex. 14.

And there is an anticipation of the mood of *Savitri* in the floating sixths of the hidden chorus of sopranos and altos representing the voice of the Earth:

Ex. 15.

It is in such moments as these that Holst's seriousness of purpose shines through the absurd conglomeration of trappings in the opera, holding fast to the greatness of the underlying idea that a god must become man before he can save the world from evil.

The year after he had finished *Sita* he began work on the settings for solo voice and piano of his own translations of hymns from the *Rig Veda*. He was still groping his way through a tangle of technical problems, struggling not to lose sight of the economy he had learnt from folk-songs in his attempts to reach the vastness of thought in these Sanskrit hymns. He was no longer satisfied with the *Invocation to Dawn* of five years ago: in the new version the waltzing three-four gives way to the instinctive length and stress of the spoken phrase. This subtler response to the rhythm of words helped more than anything else to draw him away from borrowed romanticism and to lead him towards his own natural austerity. In *Varuna* (Sky) he suddenly emerges into the clear light of his most mature thought. Bare fourths and fifths over a held pedal intersperse the silences, conveying a static aloofness:

Ex. 16.

Varuna shows that he was learning to free his harmonies from their former associations: the curving whole-tone line, 'as flies the bird unto his nest', has no suggestion of a dominant seventh in its chord of $C_1 B\flat_1 F\flat$—a faint ripple disturbs the aloof spaces for an instant, until the $F\flat$ sinks to $E\flat$, restoring the calm of the opening.

But he was not always so secure: the hymn to *Indra* (Storm and Battle) has an air of false assertion clinging to its 'Noblest of songs for the noblest of Gods!' Alas, it is a second-hand sort of nobility, and it was to lead him astray on several occasions during the next sixteen years. He was on safer ground when the words were grotesque. In the *Song of the Frogs* there is a glimpse of a scherzando frame of mind that is often found in his later works:

Ex. 17.

Where the words of the hymns expressed his own philosophy, the sheer strength of his conviction compelled him to find an adequate outline for the rise and fall of his phrases. But in working out the problems of harmony he was hampered by his lack of technique. In *Creation*, the opening declamation for unaccompanied voice is as impressive as anything he had yet written. The mood of this early song is already stretching out towards the *Betelgeuse* of twenty years later:

> Then, Life was not! Non-life was not!
> No vast expanse of air,
> Nor vaster realm of sky that lies beyond,
> No change of day and night . . .

The trouble begins at 'Then up rose Desire', for at that moment the piano accompaniment rises up on an arpeggio, and from then onwards it is a losing battle against banality. It was not just a temporary defeat—this particular problem was one that plagued him throughout most of his life. As long as he was dealing with the vastness of space his thought remained clear and undismayed. But dealing with desire was a very different matter.

These solo hymns from the *Rig Veda* cost him many painful struggles, but they helped to achieve the miracle of his one-act opera, *Savitri*. It was written in 1908, two years after *Sita* had been finished. Remembering the colossal extravagance of *Sita* with its three long acts, its large orchestra, and its paraphernalia of chariots with winged horses, it is startling to turn to the first page of the new opera and read:

Savitri.

An episode from the Mahabharata.

Characters:—Satyavan (A woodman) Tenor.
             Savitri (His wife)   Soprano.
             Death   Bass.

Scene: A wood at evening.

Time of performance: 30 minutes.

Note:—This piece is intended for performance in the open air, or else in a small building. When a Curtain is used, it should be raised before the voice of Death is heard. No Curtain, however, is necessary.

The Orchestra consists of two string quartets, a contrabass, two flutes, and an English Horn. There is also a hidden chorus of female voices. They are to sing throughout to the sound of 'u' in 'sun'.

It is a complete revolution. The size of the orchestra is astonishing enough, but perhaps the most illuminating sentence of all is the remark that 'No curtain is necessary'. He was not only throwing overboard the red glow of the sunset and all the other clap-trap; he was prepared to do without the last bulwark of theatrical make-believe. He had discovered that he had got to rely on his own words and music to create his atmosphere, as Purcell had relied on his score when he wrote 'Dido and Aeneas' for a girls' school in Chelsea, and as the 'Three Marys' had relied on their plainsong when, seven hundred years before Purcell, they had stepped into the nave of their cathedral and had sung their story to the earliest audience in Europe.

Holst was justified in doing without his curtain. His genius for economy can be recognized in the very first notes of the opera:

Ex. 18.

This opening, sung unaccompanied by an unseen voice to an empty stage, is so dramatic that it jerks the listener out of his attitude of polite curiosity into the discomfort of a sudden awareness. When Death goes on to sing: 'I am he who leadeth men onward', the unaccompanied recitative is complete in itself, implying its harmonies within the shape of its own tune. The balance of tonality in these twenty-five bars has all the assurance of his mature technique: seen through the eye, the declamation appears to fluctuate between A minor, F minor, and G♯ minor, but its sound conveys no suggestion of manœuvring from one key to another, and the enharmonic change between G♯ and A♭ takes on a relationship that has never known a text-book modulation.

When Savitri appears, and tries to shut out the sound of Death's voice, her whisper of fear echoes the line of his phrases, but with the breathlessness of human foreboding instead of the unhurried deliberation of Death. She is still muttering her fears while Death's voice grows fainter in the distance:

Ex. 19.

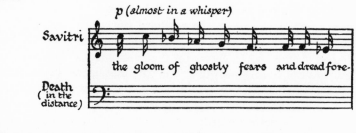

Never before had Holst written such counterpoint as this. The voices keep their independent line of thought but are drawn together by a subtle harmonic relationship: Death's G♯ on the word 'breaketh' helps to lead Savitri back into A minor before it melts on to an A♭, and at 'the song of thousands' the implied major tenth moving on to a minor third foreshadows the polytonal works of more than twenty years later. The desolation of the augmented fourth of Savitri's 'a thing of naught' is balanced by the calm inevitability of Death's rising gesture from A♭ to A♮ at 'the gate that opens for all'. Linked with the remembered D of Savitri's last note, this word 'all' draws the whole dialogue together, resolving its conflicts in the timeless indifference of a perfect fourth.

The orchestra has been silent throughout this opening scene: its first entry, on the solo viola, has the effect of transforming the orchestral players into dramatic characters who are essential to the story. A solo cello first tells us Satyavan is on his way home: he himself does not appear for some time: he sings off-stage in the distance, and all action is centred in Savitri's attitude of listening. This concentration on listening is of vital importance in the structure of the opera. Everything must be imagined, and the audience is never allowed to sink into a coma of acquiescence.

Satyavan's unaccompanied song is the only obvious example of the influence of folk music in the whole work. But there is no suggestion of 'As I walked out one May morning' about it, nor does it conjure up any visions of an English country-side. The lesson of folk-song had gone far deeper than that, guiding Holst towards an emotional restraint which reflected, in its own way, something of the non-attachment of Hindu philosophy.

When Satyavan tells Savitri that she is under the spell of Maya, or illusion, the whole forest answers him. Hidden sopranos and altos hold pianissimo chords alternating between $FA\flat C^1$ and $EA\natural C\sharp^1$, while muted solo strings tremolo from one chord to the other, creating that insubstantial world of sound which was to reach still further into the distance in *Neptune*.

Satyavan helps to explain the contrast between the simplicity of *Savitri* and the lush extravagance of *Sita*, when he says that 'our limbs, our very thoughts, we ourselves are slaves to Maya'. He is in disguise as a human, but, endowed with such a philosophy as this, he is compelled to utter his thoughts with reasonable dignity. The hero in *Sita*, although he was supposed to be a reincarnation of Vishnu, was jealous by nature, and was apt to emit such unfortunate remarks as 'Tell me but one thing, say that thou lovest me!' Sita herself, although she was the daughter of the Earth Goddess, was not intelligent enough to avoid being fooled by a scheming rival, while at one moment she stoops to the unforgivable crime of admitting: 'I am only a poor, weak woman.' Savitri would never have said that. She is inspired throughout, and although Holst's libretto has its weak moments, they are the weaknesses of a faulty craftsmanship in the language of words. There is nothing weak in the conception of the drama, and, up to this point, there has been a radiance in every note of the music. But the radiance is lost when Satyavan asks if anything in life is free from illusion, and answers, *con larghezza*: 'Love to the lover.' Holst had not learned to express such personal emotion in his new-found language, and these few bars strike an incongruous attitude. The interruption is only for an instant: the music straightens itself out to its natural height at the death of Satyavan, and Savitri's 'I am with thee, my arms are round thee', is one of the moments of great and lasting beauty in the work. There is another unforgettable moment when she astonishes Death by greeting him with courtesy instead of with fear, inviting him into her home. The sounds dissolve into a shimmering haze as the flute blends with the floating unseen voices before soaring out of their reach. But the beauty of this passage does not depend so much on the background of gossamer threads as on the utter simplicity of Savitri's 'Welcome, Lord'. This was Holst's own attitude: when she refers to death as 'our only sure possession', she is echoing his own philosophy.

But there are unfortunate modulations ahead: tunes that were first sung unaccompanied are now fettered to clinging harmonies, and there is no longer a sense of space when Death sings 'I am he that leadeth men onward'. In the passionate dialogue between Savitri and Death, when he offers to grant her anything she asks except the life of Satyavan, Holst's only tools for working up an emotional climax are his worn-out sequences of diminished sevenths and added sixths. Savitri's plea for life in its fullness is soon drowned in the borrowed sentimentality of 'the joy of striving . . . where defeat and despair are reigning', and there is an embarrassingly heroic fervour about her declamation that 'Life is communion. Each one that liveth, liveth for all.' The music that underlines these assertions sounds forced and unnatural. This is not the real Holst; it is the immature Holst who had listened to William Morris talking about Socialism and who had read Walt Whitman's appeal for a world-embracing brotherhood of man. He was still a long way from the vision of *The Hymn of Jesus* and the exaltation of 'yours is the passion of man that I go to endure'.

The music recovers its lost greatness after Death realizes that he has been defeated by the strength of Savitri's love. Nothing interferes with the beauty of the end of the opera, as Savitri tells the newly released Satyavan that one of the Holy Ones has visited them and blessed them. For an instant the air is once more filled with the shimmering other-world harmonies. Then Death, wrapped in his own darkness, passes across the stage on the way back to his Kingdom 'where men dream that they are dead, for even death is Maya'.

A performance of *Savitri* can never sound completely satisfying. The patches of imitation romanticism stand out in violent contrast to the austere economy of the work. It is impossible to consider it as a period piece, for it has moments that are as mature as anything he wrote in the last years of his life. It can only be cherished as a miraculous lesson he learnt in 1908, a lesson that helped in the slow and painful coming to birth of the new music.

The *Choral Hymns from the Rig Veda* seldom reach the height of the greatest moments in *Savitri*, but they contain the essential ingredients of much of Holst's later music. The first indications of a thought that lasted to the end of his life can be recognized in the chanting of the hymn *To the Unknown God*, where the natural freedom of the words has an underlying pulse from which there can be no escape:

Ex. 20.

The procession which follows has the same solemn tread that was first heard in the slow movement of the *Cotswolds Symphony*:

Ex. 21.

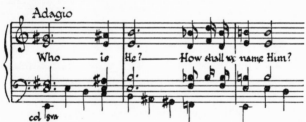

Later, he takes the augmented second and uses it in canon:

Ex. 22.

Here he is already feeling his way towards the dark immensity of the *Choral Fantasia*. (Compare Ex. 77.)

It is in the *Rig Veda* that he first makes use of a rapid and insistent five-four: the *Battle Hymn* anticipates *Mars* in its deliberate repeated crotchets and its clashing triads of F♯ and B♭. In the female voice hymn *To Agni, God of Fire*, the quick five-four rhythm leaps with abandon from one unrelated chord to another, as it changes from 3+2 to 2+3. Stressed by the tambourine, the repeated fortissimo triads move to the same pattern he afterwards uses for the dance in *The Hymn of Jesus*.

There is also a hint of *The Hymn of Jesus* in the *Funeral Chant*, when, out of the stillness, the tranquil lift of the tritones leads him to a discord that holds within its four notes the promise of that prolonged hush on 'wisdom':

Ex. 23.

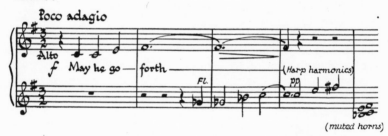

Another tranquil rising phrase that haunted him throughout his life is heard for the first time in the *Hymn to the Dawn*, where the soaring fifths stretch upwards and open a door on to a world where every detail is crystal-clear in the frostiness of suspense:

Ex. 24.

It is the world of the *Ode on a Grecian Urn*.

The ostinato bass already showed signs of becoming a habit in the *Rig Veda* hymns. It was indispensable to him in these early attempts to achieve continuity of form, and unconsciously he may have begun to take it for granted that he would always be able to rely on its help. In the *Hymn of the Travellers*, which he thought of as a possible overture to *Savitri*, it was the ostinato that taught him how to combine an intensity of harmonic expression with an economy of structure. The god invoked in this hymn is 'the Guide of Travellers of this world and along that road leading to the next', and the harp's continuous steps from D to A travel onwards with unhurried inevitability, the chorus singing in E♭ minor, as at 'Wonder-worker, hearken', where the discord cuts across the endurance with the steel-edged urgency of its appeal, or in F♯ minor, as at 'Keep us in thy care,' where the fragile tenderness opens outwards, breathing the air of *Neptune*.

There is another suggestion of *Neptune* at the end of the hymn to the *God of the Waters*, where he achieves a sense of distance with his elusive chords. But he was not always able to sustain his aloof serenity: in this same hymn the whole-tone ground bass moves unhappily as it pulls its emasculated weight against all those peevish augmented triads. He was not yet sure of himself in his use of tritones. And he was still having to fight every inch of his way in order to free himself from an unwanted romanticism. At times he wearied of the struggle: in the male-voice *Hymn to Agni*, instead of quarrying for his own material, he used French sixths just because they happened to be lying about.

These male-voice hymns show far less critical judgement than any of the earlier groups. Perhaps it was because the struggle was at its fiercest in 1912. He had been trying for years to express what he felt by grafting his own musical ideas on to an existing harmonic scheme. As each year went by, and his mind reached farther into unexplored distances, the technical difficulties involved in the compromise became more and more of a burden.

There is the same lack of critical judgement in the *Two Eastern Pictures* by Kalidasa, for S.S.A. and harp or piano. In the exotic atmosphere of *Spring*, where 'Flaming mango branches wave To and fro with the breeze Filling our hearts with sweet love-longing', he was once more unwillingly forced into a hopeless attempt to convey that 'sick with perfume' sensation. Flaming mango branches meant nothing to him: he would have been far happier among the desolate reeds and pipy hemlock of the *Choral Symphony*.

It was to Kalidasa that he turned for the words of *The Cloud Messenger*, the last of his Sanskrit compositions, begun in 1910 and revised in 1912. While working at it, he felt certain it was the best thing he had written. But the music is nearer to *Sita* than to *Savitri*: it has many of the faults of the *Rig Veda* with an added disadvantage in its cumbersome length. He could sometimes manage to sustain the rapture of a short hymn, but he was not yet equipped for an extended work on such a scale. This is also true of his translation. There are lines in *The Cloud Messenger* that are incurably dull: 'O glorious cloud, I welcome thee. Wher'ere thou goest, lonely wives, who pine in solitude with close-bound hair, will arise and gaze along the road. Thou bringest home their absent husbands.' Much of the music is on a level with this. He has dragged us back into a region where each turn of the phrase is once more in danger of landing on the chord C♯EGB. There are the well-worn sequences that should have died with *Sita*, and a terrible mock-oriental tune for the singing maidens, and a good deal of hanging around with nothing much happening except a few pentatonic arpeggios.

Occasionally his original thought breaks out with authority: when the Cloud resembles a mountain peak 'torn from its roots and hurled onward by the wind', the dominant ninth of B♭ is torn from its roots and hurled on to a chord of A, rebounding on to G♭ over the tremolo low F that is still relentlessly thundering through the storm. There is a hint of the dance in *The Hymn of Jesus* when 'the Great God himself, whose tread shakes the mountains, descends and begins his solemn dance', and in spite of the unevenness of the writing this mood can still be traced through 'Let thy thunder . . . beat out the measure for the dancing of him who holds the three worlds in his grasp', where he is very near to ecstasy in his clash of D♯F×BE'F×'.

But these moments are rare, and the work as a whole is a dismal failure. It is no wonder that he was more depressed after the first performance than he had ever been in his life. He knew, at last, that he had got to begin all over again. His next important work was *Mars*.

CHAPTER V

SCHOOL MUSIC AND
EXPERIMENTS IN ORCHESTRATION
(1908–14)

FROM the first moment when he began teaching, Holst had to lead a double life as a composer, striving towards the expression of his own individual mind and, at the same time, writing simple music for his pupils to play and sing. This double life went on until the end. It had its occasional disadvantages, but in the early years it was the greatest blessing that could possibly have happened to him. Each new work he wrote for amateurs was a practical lesson in combining a wealth of imagination with the barest economy of notes.

While he was still working at the first set of the *Choral Hymns from the Rig Veda* he was asked to write the incidental music for a *Masque* at St. Paul's Girls' School: unfortunately the orchestra was imported for the occasion, and some of the interludes lack the saving grace of economy, but the vocal writing is simple, and the flowing tunes have an innocence that suits undeveloped voices. This same innocence can be found in some of the hymns he was commissioned to write for the newly launched English Hymnal. The critical mind may reject *In the bleak midwinter* as sentimental, but the carol singer finds it entirely satisfying. Even the patriotic unison song *O England my Country* has managed to survive as an acceptable tune, though it narrowly escapes defeat in its hackneyed cadence. He was not so sure of himself in his solo songs. *The Heart Worships* hovers between innocence and sentimentality. He wrote it at a time when his powers of discrimination could not yet be relied on: in an unpublished song of 1908 it is disconcerting to find the most appalling banalities sandwiched between the chords he afterwards used at the beginning of *Venus*.

He avoided sentimentality in his part-songs, but he was not always able to avoid the competent dullness which has a way of adhering to test pieces for musical festivals. There is far more character to be found in the *Whittier Part-Songs* for children, though the words sometimes have a dampening effect on the vitality of the music: it seems a little hard that the unfortunate schoolchildren should have to sing 'there's life alone in duty done, and rest alone in striving'.

As usual, he was at his best when writing for unaccompanied

female voices. In *The Swallow leaves her Nest* the rising phrase 'for why complain?' has a poignancy that is memorable. And in *Pastoral* the pianissimo dancing thirds have caught some of the delicate gossamer of *saltato* bowing. He had long since realized that small amateur choirs could reach an astonishingly high standard of singing if they chose music that suited them.

The lessons he had learnt in writing for children and amateurs proved helpful in his works for military band. Here his players were highly skilled experts as far as their instruments were concerned, but the music they played had to be simple and economical. The *First Suite in E♭* was an experiment in form, each movement being founded on a fragment of the opening Chaconne. He was in his second apprenticeship: having learned that symphonic development and leitmotif were equally hopeless for his sort of tune, he was trying to find a form that would satisfy his own needs, and the Chaconne proves how far he had travelled since the first years of the folk-song influence. The whole suite is superbly written for military band, especially the scherzando variation in the Intermezzo which exactly suits the brittle texture of the wood-wind. It must have been a startling change from the usual operatic selections, and there are bandsmen who still remember the excitement of the first rehearsal in 1909. In spite of its original approach, the Suite never breaks away from the essential traditions of the band, and the March is the sort of music that is beloved of bombardons and euphoniums. It was not for nothing that Holst had played trombone on the pier in his student days: when he opens out into an inevitable *meno mosso*, it is with the assurance of an experienced bandsman who knows exactly what the other players are going to enjoy.

The *Second Suite in F* for military band, written two years later, is founded on Hampshire folk-songs, and it shows that he was no longer defeated by the problem of how to avoid awkward joins when dealing with traditional tunes. In the last movement, a 'Fantasia on the Dargason', which he afterwards used as the finale to the *St. Paul's Suite* for strings, the six-eight tune travels light-heartedly with time to notice all that happens on the way, and when he combines it with 'Greensleeves' he achieves the perfect marriage of contrasted folk-tunes. It is difficult to believe the two tunes were not specially intended for each other: they live their own lives, each leaning to the other instead of fighting for their independence. It was a fortunate venture: never again did he succeed so brilliantly in this highly dangerous practice.

Beni Mora, an oriental suite for orchestra, is a long way removed from his writings for amateurs. Apart from the early *Suite* of 1900, this was his first attempt at music for entertainment, and it was not altogether a success. But it helped him to escape from the temptation of lingering too long in the vague loveliness of the Dorian mode, and it taught him a good deal about form. During a holiday in Algeria he had heard a four-note tune played on a bamboo flute for $2\frac{1}{2}$ hours on end, and in the third dance in *Beni Mora* this same tune is repeated at an unvaried level of pitch for 163 bars. Considerable ingenuity was needed to prevent his listeners from becoming frantic about half-way through. The work is a skilful experiment in a foreign idiom. He was to make many such experiments during his life, which is perhaps why one critic has referred to his style as 'a compendium or *pastiche* of the styles of nearly all representative modern composers'. But it is not the desperate borrowing of a man who is short of ideas; it is the determined search of a man who knows he can write imitation folk-music but who has made up his mind not to repeat himself. His own individual thought can be recognized in the first few bars, when the rhapsodic opening for strings is unexpectedly punctuated by clucking staccato discords on trumpet and trombones, and in the Second Dance when the violas divide into three and imitate a horn-call, their triads shifting from C to B over the bassoon's held A. The last few bars of this movement are feeling their way towards the end of *Uranus*, and the opening of the Third Dance foreshadows a mood of twenty years later:

Ex. 25.

The orchestration throughout *Beni Mora* was a good rehearsal for *The Planets*. It was typical of him to have cued-in his instruments so that the work could be played when half the wood-wind and brass were missing.

Several years later he again attempted to write oriental dance music in the *Japanese Suite* for orchestra. Most of it is disappointing, but

D

the Marionette Dance has an elasticity in its cross-rhythms of six-eight against three-four that shares the same freedom as *Mercury*.

He was trying out some of the possibilities for the texture of *Venus* in the *Invocation* for solo cello and small orchestra. As in the earlier *Song of the Night* for violin, the opening *senza misura* suggests that it will one day blossom into the *Lyric Movement*. But the work is not of any value in itself.

Another rehearsal for the orchestration of *The Planets* was the *Phantastes Suite*, written in 1911. The music was so bad that he withdrew it after the first performance. It was useful as an exercise in dealing with unfamiliar effects, for he indulged in such luxuries as the celesta and the bass flute, and, as in *Beni Mora*, he used his strings *col legno*. But the sounds he produced were exceedingly dreary. In a March intended to represent the Jabberwock 'whiffling through the tulgey wood', he used four horns in unison on a fortissimo marcato passage for natural harmonics, culminating in a glissando from written high G to the out-of-tune B♭ below. And he insisted on having the same passage over and over again. The noise must have sounded appalling, and long before the seventh repetition of this particular outrage the work must have suffered from the irremediable deflation of a joke that has fallen flat. In the slow movement there is an anticipation of *The Perfect Fool* ballet when the bass flute enters at its lowest register on the cadenza he afterwards uses for the invocation to the Spirits of Water. In the last movement there is a typically angular whole-tone tune like a folk-song turned sour:

Ex. 26.

Crude as it is, in its essentials it is the same voice that can be heard at the end of his life, in the *Double Concerto* and in *Hammersmith*.

Setting scenes from Greek tragedies was the next experiment he tried. *Hecuba's Lament* for alto solo, chorus of female voices, and orchestra, is a mixture of declamation in the Dorian and layers of the modulating sequences he had not yet learned to do without. The

unquenchable drama in the music pushes its way through the inadequacies: there is a stark directness in the opening recitative and in the
first entry of the chorus on a high piercing 'Woe'. But the melodramatic storm fragment leading to 'the dust as smoke riseth' is once
more a borrowed sound and fury: he had to wait another three years
before he found his own language for the storm of war. Only occasionally does he speak with such assurance as in the desolate cry after
the fall of Troy, where there is an undisguised depth and distance
and distress.

The *Hymn to Dionysus*, for female voices and orchestra, was
written two years later, in 1913. There is more sensuous sound in the
work than is usual in Holst's music. He may have been listening to
Vaughan Williams's setting of 'Where is the home for me?', one of the
choruses from the 'Bacchae' which he wrote when he was still under
the influence of his lessons from Ravel. To Holst, this brief venture
on the fringe of an impressionist world was a blessing in more ways
than one: it helped to dispel the gloom of that disastrous first performance of *The Cloud Messenger* and it made him work out some of
the harmonic progressions that he afterwards needed in *The Planets*.

The *Hymn to Dionysus* shows some of the conflicting styles that
were influencing him at this most critical stage in his development.
The unison chanting and the pentatonic ripples of sound are calm
with the sort of tranquillity that is bred of inertia and lack of
opportunity. It was a dangerous tranquillity for English music
at this time and for many years to come, and it was particularly
dangerous for Holst, whose love of the Dorian was deep-rooted and
who could easily have been led back to its soothing embrace at a
moment when he desired at all costs to avoid repeating the mistakes
of *The Cloud Messenger*. Shimmering muted strings cross and re-cross
the triad of A with an added F♯, while the horns drift through the
mist on a pianissimo rising scale. And then it begins all over again on
a foundation of D♭, with the wood-wind rippling round the added
sixth. It all sounds very pleasant, but it is the sort of thing he had no
patience with in later years. On ceasing to be sterile it becomes
squashy, as in the *espressivo* 'For her heart was dying, dying', though
it happens that during the course of these squashes he reaches an
early version of the magic chords in *Neptune*. When the dance begins
he borrows would-be oriental harmonies from the language of *Beni
Mora* and combines them with descending chromatic scales; the
mixture is confusing, but at any rate it saves the music from sinking
into a bog of pentatonic self-satisfaction. As the excitement of the

dance mounts up to 'the wild orb of our orgies,' there is a groping towards the ecstatic harmonies of *The Hymn of Jesus* in the vibrations of the timbrel, and at the galloping ride the one-in-a-bar cross-rhythms leap into the air with an urgency that lifts the listening mind:

Ex. 27.

It was some years later that he wrote his *Seven Choruses from Alcestis* for voices in unison, three flutes, and harp. The music was meant for use during a school performance of the play, and the simple tunes never lie too high for undeveloped voices. The harmonies are severely economical, achieving a darkness and dignity with the flutes' unadorned triads and the harp's bare fifths and octaves, while there are moments of great intensity at the characteristic alternation between A major and B♭ minor. Helped by the frugal texture of the accompaniment, these short choruses have a dramatic unity that is lacking in both *Hecuba's Lament* and *Dionysus*. Once again, his limited material resources proved to be his salvation.

The *Alcestis* choruses were written for his pupils at St. Paul's Girls' School, and it was for their orchestra that he wrote his *St. Paul's Suite* for strings. It is one of his happiest works. The cheerful abandon with which the Jig broadens out into augmentation and then catches up with itself shows the influence of the 'capers' in the Morris dance tunes he had recently been arranging for military band. The whole movement is harmonically very simple, although, to the ears of those who are used to conducting it with elementary orchestras, the quaver passage beginning in C♯ has acquired an unavoidable flavour of atonality that was not intended by the composer. At the end there is a faint suggestion of *Mars* as the fortissimo discord is reiterated over and over again, punctuating the dramatic silences before coming to rest on its final held C. But the drama is immeasurably slighter, and every particle of agony has been left out.

The Ostinato shows that his second apprenticeship was coming to an end. Light and effortless, the same four rapid quavers curl down and up throughout the movement. The tune for solo violin has a care-free lilt that he was not often able to achieve in later years: it succeeds in persuading him to include a rare snippet of a waltz in his skilfully varied texture. There is a foretaste of *Mercury* in the change from three-four to two-four, the pulse of the music quickening while the quavers remain at the same speed. The return to the three-four is typical: he uses his ground bass of four descending notes to work up a mock fury of anger—the fortissimo crotchets on the muted strings sound rough and comically fussy; the characteristic rising scale in quavers sweeps right through the music from the depths of the double basses' ground to high above the second violins' ostinato, and suddenly the anger and the fuss are blown away and we are back again at the three-four dance. Joins are no longer joins: they have become an integral part of the music.

The Intermezzo, with its eagerly plaintive solo for violin over pizzicato chords, transports us through the *Hymn of the Travellers* to the world of *Savitri*. The sudden interruption of the Vivace comes as a violent shock. It is the same tune he afterwards uses for the Spirits of the Fire in *The Perfect Fool* ballet; here, in the Intermezzo, it never attempts to have any dealings with the first tune, but remains a separate and disruptive element. In the last Andante he enjoys the luxury of being thoroughly ardent in octaves, and in the Coda, where the solo quartet broadens out into an Adagio, the descending chromatic sixths are like a gesture of farewell to the good old days: never again did he indulge in such an unblushing display of nineteenth-century romanticism.

The Finale is almost identical with the Fantasia on the Dargason at the end of the *Second Suite* for Military Band. The movement fits in well with the others, though an occasional passage, such as the melodramatic tremolo, comes as a reminder that the music was written three years before the rest of the suite, and that a good deal had happened to him during those three years.

It was also for his pupils at St. Paul's that he wrote *Lord who hast made us*, one of the *Two Psalms* for chorus, string orchestra, and organ. There are glimpses of beauty in the leisurely Alleluias that wander up and down in thirds while the familiar hymn tune sails over their heads, but it is the first psalm, *To my humble supplication*, that fulfils the high hopes raised by the *Four Old English Carols* of 1907. The tenor solo declaims the recitative with a passionate intensity in the rise and fall of his phrases, an intensity that has its roots in plainsong. It is answered by the unaccompanied sopranos and altos, who join the tenor at the end of each line of his prayer, gathering his words together and lifting them into the measured serenity of their harmonies. At the end there is an unforgettable moment when the violas divide on the C string for their Amen, while the pizzicato cellos and basses comment on it with the untroubled questioning of a second inversion.

This same quality of passionate intensity can be heard in every note of the *Dirge for Two Veterans*, a setting of the poem by Walt Whitman for male voices, brass, and drums. There is immense strength and dignity in that 'sad procession'—the same sad procession that never ceased to move through his mind until the very end of his life. The conviction in its relentless rhythm cuts through the last shreds of a worn-out idiom: the one conventional modulation in the cantabile passage is soon forgotten in the shudder of the convulsive drums and in the return of those questioning trumpets that were already bursting into their fiercer and more shattering challenge in *Mars*.

CHAPTER VI

THE PLANETS

(1914–17)

'As a rule I only study things that suggest music to me', Holst wrote in 1914. 'That's why I worried at Sanskrit. Then recently the character of each planet suggested lots to me.' It happened that once again he had found the right stimulus at the moment when he most needed it. Without the help of a clearly defined character for each of his seven movements it is unlikely he would have attempted to write a symphonic suite of such dimensions. He was continually being defeated by the technical problems of extended form: years later, he was still unable to grapple with the difficulties of writing a symphony. But by now he had reached the stage in his development when it was essential for him to find the courage to embark on a large-scale work. He was in his fortieth year, and his ideas were becoming more and more insistent. Suddenly, with the character of each planet suggesting a strongly contrasted mood, he was able to express these insistent ideas in music that was different from anything he had written before. This suddenness, however, was not the result of any new musical influence that had swept him off his feet; it was the result of a twenty years' search for the right idiom for what he wanted to say. Outside influences had helped. Stravinsky's music had let in a great light, and he had been impressed by a recent performance of Schönberg's Five Orchestral Pieces. But although the influence of Stravinsky is obvious, most of *The Planets* is written in Holst's own language, which had hitherto been heard in occasional snatches and isolated phrases. Now, at last, he had learned enough grammar to go ahead fearlessly into an unfamiliar region of sound.

He had begun working at *Mars*, the Bringer of War, in May 1914, and he finished the first sketch just before the war broke out. The storm that sweeps through the music is a storm in the mind. The persistent five-four of the *col legno* G strings pulls against the slow heave of the bassoons and horns as they rise from G to D and sink back, defeated, on to a Db, with a growing menace behind their crescendo and diminuendo. There is tragedy in the gap of the diminished third as the chord of Db lunges on to the chord of B, bringing with it the haunting distress of that dark step downwards in the second Kyrie of the B minor Mass: but here the distress is beyond the hope of salvation. When the repeated G moves triumphantly forward on to C it meets the violent hammering of a D♭ that knocks out all the achievement of arrival at the very first blow. The chromatic major triads sprawl across the staccato five-four, letting their weight slither down inch by inch and then heaving it up again. Each time they rise they try to get a little bit higher, before slipping all the way back and having to start all over again in their struggle against the remorseless five-four, which has now grown from a distant mutter to an imminent threat. The dotted rhythm of the legato triads is spread out in a surging five-two, characteristically extending over the bar-line and utterly disregarding it as it fills two bars with its rise and fall. These triads have nothing in common with the chromaticisms which have led him in his earlier works from one key to the next, or have coloured the harmonic progressions within the diatonic scale: here each triad is an independent link in the chain that holds the monstrous phrase together.

There is an instant's slackening of the tension when the dominant tries to assert its need for a normal healthy relationship between one chord and another, but there is no time to listen to it, for at the next moment the trumpets and tenor tuba begin their terrifying pursuit. They force their way higher at each step, from minor third to major third, from fourth to diminished fifth, while the answering voice never quite catches up. After the agony of this nightmare the disintegrating semiquavers come as a relief: even the voice of doom at the pause is a relief. The storm sinks to its lowest ebb; the chromatic rise and fall sounds desperately weary in its empty octaves. The five-four has shrunk to a shuddering low G♯ on the violins, with an occasional mutter from the side drum. This is the first time these triplets have been heard on the side drum: he gave the opening five-four to the timpani with wooden sticks, knowing their added depth would draw more weight of resistance from the *col legno* strings. Heard in slow motion, as if from a long way off, the side drum's protest is unavoidably reminiscent of the last spasmodic splutter of machine-gun firing when the brain controlling the trigger already knows the battle is lost. But *Mars* was not programme music. After two mechanized wars it would be easy to take it for granted that the work had been commissioned as background music for a documentary film of a tank battle, but Holst had never heard a machine gun when he wrote it, and the tank had not yet been invented.

The despair in the music turns to fury and the fury mounts up until it breaks out in all its old relentlessness. The howling discord hammers its way through the last few bars of the movement with a force that is cruel and calculated, while the silences between each stroke are filled with the horror of waiting for the next crash. The final pause on the bare fifth of C and G brings no comfortable assurance of an easing-off in a situation that has become unendurable. The sound is a bare statement of fact, a reminder that the two notes of its interval are the two pillars of an unchanging structure upon which all harmonic balance depends. They remain when every inessential has been blown to bits. The tension has given way to their strength: they can afford to be at rest.

For the first time in his life Holst had said what he wanted to say in a way in which only he could have said it. He had not yet grown up to his full stature, but the twenty years' apprenticeship was over.

Venus, the Bringer of Peace, has to try and bring the right answer to *Mars*. The calm notes of the solo horn rise through empty space, and the cool flutes sail down to meet them, blending with the glitter of the oboes and bringing the solace of contrary motion after so much parallel surging up and down. As they draw inwards the listener sighs with relief to hear them come to rest for a while in the safe anchorage of their minor triad. When the air stirs it is with the movement of quietly undulating crotchets that change to and fro over repeated chords on flutes and horns and harps, while a low sustained pedal note stretches out to hold their vibrations.

And then we are pulled down to earth by a cello arpeggio that sounds as if it has strayed from its appropriate surroundings. Back in the insecurity of an *espressivo*, Holst is led into perilously romantic modulations at the animato. It was one of his bad habits at this time, and for some years afterwards, that whenever he was not quite sure of himself—either at a difficult bit of a join or at some emotionally embarrassing moment when he was tied up with his harmonies—he would put in a poco accelerando, as if he were nervously trying to get over the ground as soon as possible.

The oboe solo at the Largo is in the nature of a swan-song: it is almost the last time he allows himself to indulge in the luxury of a sweetness that was soon to become intolerable. He had to wait until the last years of his life before he could bring himself to return to these sweeping melodic sixths in the Nocturne of the *Moorside Suite* and in the *Lyric Movement*.

This is the least convincing section of *Venus*, with its short fragments of animated modulation strung together between two or three bars of a *Largo con espressione* tune that becomes more and more *espressivo* each time it occurs. But although it is unconvincing, some such breaking up of the tranquillity was essential, in order that the listener might be able to welcome the calm return of the opening. *Neptune* can exist in unbroken quietness, but *Venus* has neither the depth nor the economy of *Neptune*.

In *Mercury*, the Winged Messenger, his technique keeps pace with his imagination. He could feel thoroughly at home in such a scherzo as this, where his swiftly moving thought could delight in the fantastic unexpectedness of a restless leggiero. And here, for the first time in his works, he sets out to experiment in bitonality. There had been instances of bitonal harmony in his earliest compositions, but they were the rare dazzling chords which had come together in the excitement of the moment without realizing what they were about: after their brief flash of ecstasy they invariably returned to their law-abiding surroundings. In *Mercury*, with the lightest possible touch, he deliberately divides the particles of his phrase into separate keys and then listens to them swiftly joining together again. The broken chord of the second inversion of B♭ is caught and linked up with the descending three quavers of the first inversion of E, and the fragments dart to and fro, scattered over the whole range of wood-wind and muted strings, and pricked out by staccato first inversions. The mixed scale that begins in B♭ and goes on in E has hardly had time to run uphill through several octaves before the listening ear is ready to accept it as one scale. It is answered by the pricking first inversions, the rhythm of their two-bar phrases of six-eight crotchets giving the impression of fluctuating between six-four and three-two. These frequent changes are as free as air, and the tune at ③ has such extreme elasticity that it gives the impression of containing an uneven number of beats. He had rehearsed this texture in the third dance of *Beni Mora*, in the Ostinato of the *St. Paul's Suite*, and in the Marionette Dance in the *Japanese Suite*, and now that the moment has arrived he is thoroughly sure of himself. He skims over the recapitulation with alacrity, pausing in suspense on the ironical question-mark of the chord B♭ꜛꜛ F ꜛ B♭ꜛ E♮, and splitting it into tentative quavers on the bass oboe and the English horn: the particles of sound run together on the same ironical pause and then suddenly we are back at the beginning again.

There is the rushing of the wind in the muted strings' rising quavers, breaking into a violent spurt of energy as the wood-wind joins in:

Ex. 28.

Throughout *Mercury*, the orchestration has the clarity and lightness of a string quartet. But this is not chamber-music: it needs the enormous body of muted strings to achieve the effect of those buffeting currents of air.

Jupiter was intended to be the Bringer of Jollity, but although Holst had an abundance of good humour in his own nature, he was not yet able to express it in his music. At the opening, which is built up on familiar bustling fourths with a shifting stress in their repeated time-pattern, the very first tune sounds forced:

Ex. 29.

The syncopation is calculated rather than felt; it would be impossible to move to it with the effortless abandon of a Purcell hornpipe, where the return to the pulse is always instinctively at the right moment for the dancer to adjust the weight of his body. *Jupiter* was not meant to be a dance, but the listener experiences a physical sensation of being left hitched-up by the unnatural delay in Ex. 29. It is the first of many irritations, such as the angular insistence of the trumpet-call, the banal repetition of the cadence that follows it, and the frequent attempts to work up the climaxes by repeating what has been said before but saying it louder and quicker. The pesante tune at ③ is clumsily cheerful, but the repeated fragments never achieve anything beyond staggering downhill in a staccato dominant thirteenth, which, with the help of a chromatic lurch from the tuba, lands us just where we started, without having had any real enjoyment out of the twelve bars. The mock folk-tune at ⑤ sounds more like Holst, but he uses it over and over again without any feeling of organic growth to justify so much repetition.

Among the many jokes that fail to come off, perhaps the most irritating of all is the deliberately flattened seventh in the cadence before the big tune: it still persists in sounding like an uncorrected mistake in the orchestral parts. This maestoso tune belongs to Holst's 'other life' of school-singing and Morley College festivities. It is a real tune, whether one likes it or not. Unfortunately it is nearly always associated with the hymn *I vow to thee, my country*, owing to the fact that he used it as a setting to these words some years afterwards, against his better judgement, when overwork had reduced him to a condition in which he was unable to sit down and write even a short commission. It is impossible to prevent an aura of patriotism from hovering over a large section of the audience at this moment in *The Planets*: backs become visibly straighter; minds that may have been wandering in a maze of flippant irrelevancies come to attention with a shock and prepare themselves for what they consider to be an appropriate state of reverence. But alas, nothing could be less appropriate. The abrupt breaking off and the frivolous comments of the wood-wind are enough to prove that when Holst first wrote that tune he had no idea there would ever be anything solemn about it.

The many weak moments in *Jupiter* show how much he still had to learn about form. Irretrievably linked to the weaknesses in construction are the ill-placed moments of rubato: there is a distressing vulgarity about the *Meno mosso . . . accel . . . a tempo* at ⑬. It might not be so bad if all the jokes were meant to be grotesque, but Holst had had no intention of creating a monster: he had been working at Handel's 'L'Allegro' with his Morley College choir and orchestra, and he had hoped that *Jupiter* was going to represent 'laughter holding both his sides'. But it was beyond him.

After the blatancy of *Jupiter* it is like breathing another atmosphere to enter the vast cold regions of *Saturn*, the Bringer of Old Age. This is Holst's own sort of music. He is so completely immersed in its mood that all problems of technique vanish and the form unfolds with the unhurried inevitability of approaching old age, each note changing place with the last and tirelessly counting out the minutes as they pass by.

Ex. 30.

Here is the desolation which followed him, years afterwards, into that other bleak expanse of *Egdon Heath*. The to and fro of the repeated ninths conveys an aloofness to the slow tread of the minims, and the hollow tolling of the flutes and harps is weighed down by the indifference of the augmented fourths. Out of these two chords he builds the sentence that haunts the whole of the movement. There is little flesh on the bones of this tune when it is first heard on the double-basses: the violins and violas, echoing the rise and fall of the semitone on the G string, drew it out in a long crescendo from *pp* to *f* and back again, hinting at endless possibilities of woe: the oboe adds its melancholy comment, followed by the thin, high voice of the cello, the despairing notes of the bass oboe, and the horn's resignation. It is the same short phrase, but there is a different world of experience behind each entry.

At ⒈ we hear the 'sad procession' moving to the burden of the pizzicato crotchets of the cellos and basses. The trombones' dirge is founded on the phrase in Ex. 30 but it has left the aloof distances and has shrunk to a human tragedy. When it gives way to that other, remoter procession, there is an unearthly quality in the low notes of the four flutes as they move from one common chord to the next, each step echoed by the tread of the syncopated harps and pizzicato

basses and timpani: it is a tread that counts the clock with remorseless
regularity. The steps come nearer as the brass joins the procession,
leaning heavily on every note, and there is a moment of panic when
the bells suddenly begin clanging out the notes of foreboding that
were heard long ago in the quiet opening. The whole orchestra clashes
with them, as if their metallic insistence had drawn a vibrating response
from every instrument. The opening tune, with its depth of tragic
devastation, can be heard through all the clangour; it is answered
by the passionate protest of the solo trumpet, and the agony is
intensified at the climax four bars later:

Ex. 31.

But there is more than protest in this climax: it is the moment of
arrival and it implies acceptance. From now onwards the bells become
intermittent, slowing down and sounding farther and farther away
until they melt into the distant ninths, while the air still heaves with
the vibrations of those past clashes.

A change comes over the music when the tranquillo harp harmonics
are heard in a chime that holds no memory of panic: the descending
four notes, phrased over the three-two bar-line, are like a peaceful
comment on the ostinato of the sad procession.

The double-basses return to their first phrase of Ex. 30, but all the
anguish has gone, for the augmented fourth has become perfect and
the minor second has become major and there is no crescendo. The
harps have also had the sting of despair taken out of them: all anxiety
melts away until there is a suggestion of tenderness in the dominant
ninth at twelve bars after ⑤. As the chimes dissolve into shimmering
ripples of sound, the six horns carry their notes calmly to and fro,
with a gesture that resembles Savitri's welcome to Death, when she
says that 'the air itself is holy'. The tranquil double-bass tune has
stretched its way across all the strings and is now untroubled by any
recollection of despair; the air thins out and gets clearer and rarer,
leaving the flutes to echo the horns' chiming until they, too, are lost

in the distance and only the strings are left on a high held first inversion of E minor. It is the right sound for the mood of acceptance, bringing the movement to an end on a question that has little need of an answer.

The peaceful resignation of *Saturn* is shattered by the violent shock of the first four notes of *Uranus*, the Magician:

Ex. 32.

This angular incantation on fortissimo trumpets and trombones is strident with derision, as if it were mocking the underlying harmonies of Ex. 30. Holst is back again in a region of wizards and their magic spells, and we are made to suffer from some of the blatancies that were left over when *Phantastes* was discarded. The Magician's borrowed apprentices hop about in a galumphing six-four; and the flavour of a parody persists, causing an unfounded but horrible suspicion that the staccato trumpets and xylophone are trying to burlesque the tolling of Saturn's approach with their mocking cross-rhythm of three-two against six-four.

The tune at ② is typical of Holst in this mood: with grotesque clumsiness he chops it up into sequences and 'develops' it in true text-book style, adding to the confusion of the situation. At ③ the tune is a mixture of mock-oriental and mock folk-song, with a flat-footed accompaniment that gets heavier and noisier at each repetition. It is followed by several bars of true comedy as the timpani quotes the galumphing six-four version of the incantation, and the bass tuba replies with the original slow notes of Ex. 32 which it utters in a subdued and pensive tone of voice, provoking the two piccolos to let out a high shriek that is echoed all the way down the flutes and clarinets.

The Magician's amateurish incompetence can be recognized in the preposterous bit of padding sixteen bars after ⑥ and in the growing caution of his long-drawn-out rallentando before ⑦ . The noise after this is terrific: with the full orchestra going at it hammer and tongs it seems certain that something will burst before long, and just as it is getting unbearable, the organ glissando sweeps everything away, transporting us into a region that has never known make-

believe, where magic itself stares down unblinking from a million
miles away:

Ex. 33.

When the first harp enters this hush, its restatement of the incantation is far removed from all human comment. For an instant there
is a bustle of activity among the scattered remains of the magician's
workshop: the bassoons try and pick up the pieces of the apprentices'
dance, and the tubas let out an expletive over the incantation that
has failed them. But it is no good: the answer comes back emphati-
cally at ⑨. Echoes of this magic chord are washed up one after
another until the strings are left alone, holding the *ppp* vibrations
of the crash while the first harp repeats its remote statement. It gets
as far as the third note and then waits: there is a moment of breathless
suspense while the air is still quivering with the last remnants of
that drowned chord, and then the second harp provides the subtly
ironical resolution of the low fifth on E and B. It is worth going
through all the noise and stridency to arrive at these last twenty-
eight bars.

The quiet ending of *Uranus* is not so distant as the quieter opening
of *Neptune*, the Mystic. A footnote in the score says that in *Neptune*
'the orchestra is to play sempre *pp* throughout', and in Holst's own
copy he has added in pencil: '*dead* tone, except the clarinet after ⑤.'
It is not the dead hush of despair: it is the intense concentration of a
prolonged gaze into infinity. The mind is emptied of all memory of
bitter frustration and of the soothing calm that followed it: there is
no need now for the swiftness of thought to pierce the distance, nor
for the sense of well-being to distract the mind from its vastness.
Old age has long since ceased to matter. The vision has stretched far
beyond the limits of time and space, and the fantastic attempts to
force an entry into that other world are soon forgotten.

Holst matches the intensity of the mystic's gaze with the economy of his music. The whole of *Neptune* moves round the alternating chords of E minor and G♯ minor: they change place with the effortless hush of calm deep breathing, the E minor chord lasting a dotted minim and the G♯ minor a minim. The tension and relaxation are ironed out so smoothly that they are almost imperceptible. There is no shadow of anxiety, no hint of stress about this pulse that moves so faintly: but the pulse is there, and the long breathe-in and the shorter breathe-out are sufficient to keep the music flowing. The opening sixths on the lowest register of the flute and bass flute are calmer than anything that has yet been heard in *The Planets*. There is a trembling in the air as the harps are drawn in on their high shimmering triad of G♯ minor. The sound continues through the long breathe-in of the flutes' E minor sixths, hinting at those dazzling distances that are waiting to enfold the mind as it stretches out to meet them. Soon the intake of each breath becomes a mingling of E minor and G♯ minor; when the two chords 'resolve', their only movement is to change places with each other. Later, the harps cross and recross in floating arpeggios of E minor with an added D♯: poised between the two harmonies, this D♯ links them still more closely. As the quaver sixths dissolve into semiquavers and demisemiquavers, the ripples of sound spread farther and farther into the air, filling vast empty spaces with their vibrations. There is no monotony, for the balance is perfectly adjusted. When the chords change to B minor over E♭ minor they convey no suggestion of journeying from the tonic to the dominant: the bitonality prevents the progression from intruding any familiar outlines of shape into this haze of sound. The relationship is stated in the aloof, impersonal language of *Neptune*, and is accepted without any emotional or intellectual repercussions. The blend of the two keys casts such a spell over the ear that when the music arrives at a rippling chord of B♭ major over a held E♭ pedal it sounds stranger than the most unfamiliar of discords: it is as if one had never heard B♭ and E♭ together before in any other connexion. There is nothing sensuous about the strings' *sul pont.* tremolo or the harps' ethereal glissandos, for their tone is still 'dead': any leanings towards an *espressivo* would bring a richness into the music that would overload it with intolerable longing, shattering the timeless atmosphere and destroying the concentration of the vision. At 5 the haze clears, leaving only the low held notes of the strings. It is a hush of expectancy, but there can be no question of a recapitulation, for there has been no development: the rippling waves have spread farther but there has been no struggle and therefore there is no need

for a reconciliation. No peaceful return is possible, for the peace has
never left us. And so we never hear any more of those quietly moving
sixths on the flutes. What we hear is the broken chord of E minor,
with a supertonic passing-note that has already been hinted at as long
ago as ⒊, rising in calm allegretto crotchets, floating upwards over
the held first inversion of E major, and forming triads as it journeys
on its way. When the long-held G♯ in the bass curls upwards on
to an A, it hints at the faint possibility of a dominant, and brings,
for the first time, a touch of warmth into the music. It is like a far-off
memory of the welcome of old age in *Saturn* and the welcome of
death in *Savitri*: but we are beyond time and space, and the greeting
cannot be for either of them. The mood persists, and the listener
gradually realizes that there are voices singing a high G, effortlessly
sustained. At first it is difficult to believe that the ear is not imagining
the sound. But the note becomes clearer, and the tenderness increases
as the clarinet draws the deadness into a dolce that leads to the
singers' flowing canon. Soon the music reaches the 'Neptune'
harmonies of B♯ minor followed by C♯ minor over a held E and B.
For an instant the sound dissolves into shimmering arpeggios. Then
the hidden voices are left alone, singing their last two chords over
and over again until their notes are lost in the distance:

Ex. 34.

There can be no coming to an end on that tideless sea of sound.

Listening to *The Planets* is a perplexing experience. The work is
so uneven that it is almost impossible to believe the same mind was
responsible for the whole of the fifty-five minutes of music. Many
critics, suffering acutely from the pain inflicted by its weakest
moments, find it difficult to tolerate the work, and protest that it is
nothing but a 'mausoleum'. But it has not sunk to such depths as that.
The great moments survive in spite of the irrelevancies that surround
them. It would be useless to try and disguise the unevenness of the
work by leaving out the worst bits: a performance of *Mars, Mercury,*

Saturn, and *Neptune* would be just as mistaken as the occasional execrable habit of playing *Venus*, *Jupiter*, and *Uranus*. The seven movements are necessary to each other, not only because of their contrasting moods but also because of the inter-related rhythms and harmonies that link one planet with the next. It is unlikely that Holst deliberately thought out these relationships: augmentation over the bar-line and three-four against six-eight were habits of mind that insisted on making themselves heard in one movement after another. Nor would it be wise to get unduly excited at finding *Neptune*'s elusive harmonies fluttering their way through *Mercury*'s message in Ex. 28 or confronting *Uranus* in the remote gaze of Ex. 33. These sounds lay at the farthest margin of his voyage of discovery: they haunted him until they were left behind on the next outward journey.

Holst never considered that *The Planets* was one of his best works, and it distressed him when it became a popular success. But he liked *Saturn*, and he was glad to have learnt so much from having written the other movements.

CHAPTER VII

MUSIC FOR THAXTED

(1916–17)

HE had begun *The Planets* in the spring of 1914 and it was not until early in 1917 that he finished scoring the whole suite, working at week-ends and throughout the month of August, which was the only time he had for his own compositions during those two and a half years. He was spending more and more of his energy in teaching school-children to sing folk-songs and in rehearsing Bach cantatas with his amateur choirs and orchestras. He was also writing easy music for them to sing and play, which meant that he was unconsciously bridging the gap between the contemporary composer and that mythical being known as 'the ordinary listener'. Holst's ordinary listeners could all sing or play after a fashion, and they were ready to approach an unfamiliar work with enthusiastic determination, whether it was written in 1915 or in 1591. He never realized he was helping to restore some of the lost balance of supply and demand between the composer and the public. He had no theories about such matters: teaching had become part of his life, and it was inevitable that he should compose for his pupils.

He had been writing *The Planets* during the long week-ends he spent in a small cottage at Thaxted, in Essex, and while he was there he managed to find time to train the members of the choir to sing Byrd and Palestrina in their beautiful church. Thaxted was the right place for his sort of music-making: the vicar was a socialist with a sense of humour, and the singers phrased their unaccompanied plainsong with tremendous conviction. Soon Holst was able to bring some of his pupils from Morley College and St. Paul's Girls' School to combine with the Thaxted choir in Bach and Purcell at a Whitsun festival. This was the beginning of a tradition that brought immeasurable joy into his life, making him realize 'why the bible insists on heaven being a place where people sing and *go on singing*'.

It was for a Whitsun festival at Thaxted that he wrote his unaccompanied motet, *This have I done for my true love*, a setting of a medieval Cornish poem:

> To-morrow shall be my dancing day,
> I would my true love did so chance

To see the legend of my play,
To call my true love to the dance.
Sing O my love,
This have I done for my true love.

Ever since the years of his Sanskrit studies he had known about the close connexion between dancing and mystic ritual. And now, in 1916, when he found the words of this traditional carol copied out on a sheet of paper just inside the door of Thaxted church, he began a search for other dancing hymns, a search that led him to the apocryphal acts of St. John and *The Hymn of Jesus*. The tune he wrote for *This have I done* gives the impression of having grown with the words as if it had always belonged to them; in his setting he manages to unfold the drama without losing the continuity of the dance. The sudden change of key after the scourging might have defeated him three or four years before this, when he would probably have felt compelled to modulate his way from B minor to C minor. But by now he was learning to turn a deaf ear to the stray appeals for conventional modulation that still beset him at odd moments. This motet was the first choral work he wrote after the republication of the Tudor madrigals; strengthened by the living examples of contrapuntally harmonic daring in the music of Byrd and Weelkes, he moves freely from one unrelated chord to another, always keeping in mind the needs of his singers. His experience with elementary choirs helped him to achieve the feeling of depth and deadness at 'Then down to hell I took my way'; by giving this line to the sopranos instead of the altos he was certain of getting an expressionless tone, for it lies below the level of the sopranos' true compass, whereas it would have been difficult to persuade the altos to keep the warmth out of their voices. There is a glowing conviction in the music as the triumphant line 'and rose again' is carried into the dancing Allegretto at 'Then up to heaven I did ascend', reaching its climax in the sweeping clashes of the six-part chorus at 'Sing O my love', where the block harmonies are treated contrapuntally, their chiming first inversions crossing and recrossing in a blaze of exaltation.

The influence of the Elizabethans can be heard in the *Six Choral Folk-Songs*, where he is far happier than in his earlier piano arrangements. He had not yet found complete security; there are several of those dangerously abrupt changes of tempo that can wreck the simplicity of a folk-song, and in the *Song of the Blacksmith* the hammering of the staccato fourths and fifths does not suit the unaccompanied voices as well as it suited the wood-wind and brass in the *Second Suite for Military Band.* But in most of the settings the choral writing is unforced. The quiet persistence of the sopranos' and altos' curving phrase in *I love my love* binds the whole story together: there is a realistic anxiety in the tenors' and basses' chromatic storm at sea in *Swansea Town,* and a dateless melancholy in the fall of the flattened supertonic in *Matthew, Mark.*

He knew where he was with short settings for unaccompanied voices, but he was defeated when he tried to turn folk-songs into a *Phantasy String Quartet.* Here his attempt to combine a six-eight jig with a five-four love-song 'works' on paper, but it is fussy and has none of the freedom of the *St. Paul's Suite.* The quartet sounds as if it had been written by a young and inexperienced student who had lost his heart to folk-tunes but could do nothing with them beyond labelling them with the long-suffering title of 'Phantasy', and hoping it would cover a multitude of inadequacies. He withdrew the work from his list of compositions soon after he had written it, and having realized that this was the wrong way to use traditional tunes, he went back to his amateur singers and players, giving them exactly what they wanted in his *Three Festival Choruses.* There is no trace of the sort of counterpoint that only works on paper in *Let all mortal flesh keep silence:* the canon flows through the orchestra like an out-pouring of endless Alleluias. In *A Festival Chime,* which began life as 'Our church-bells at Thaxted', the varied chimes are never too complicated for a small village choir, and the verse for trebles only, with legato thirds over alternating tonic and dominant, is an example of a simplicity that knew how to be gracious. He was incapable of committing the crime of writing down to his amateurs, and in *Turn Back, O Man* he never allows his imagination to be pushed aside by the technical limitations of his singers. This was perhaps one of his most far-reaching contributions to the musical life of England during the difficult first quarter of the century, this reminder that the fundamental necessities of music are shared alike by the original thinker piercing the distances and by the amateur struggling to learn his notes. In *Turn Back, O Man* the pizzicato ground bass contains the whole mood of the hymn within its four descending notes: when the wood-wind and brass are heard, it is with characteristic repeated triads, their first entry on the tonic chord of G coinciding with the F♯ of the ground bass and conveying in the very simplest terms the underlying warning of conflict. It is also with the simplest possible means that he suggests the depth of desolation at 'Age after age her tragic empires rise': the low-lying clarinets and bassoons add their doomed and deserted melancholy to the tenors and basses whose singing has been drained dry by the absence of any hint of a crescendo. Choirs often insist on getting louder here, being carried away by the emotion of the moment, and refusing to believe that the composer would not allow them to warm up on their rising phrase. But Holst, as usual, knew exactly what he wanted, and when his singers and players do what he asks of them, the hymn stretches out towards the mood of that 'sad procession' in *Saturn*. The music has a greatness that is lacking in the later and more ambitious *Festival Te Deum*: in *Turn Back, O Man* he is safe from all temptations; even the accelerando in the third verse, which might have grown perilously near to melodrama, sweeps securely through the rising scales, carrying the wave of sound from one voice to another and bursting into the last verse where the trumpets' repeated triads are a reassurance and the ostinato is no longer tragic but triumphant. The work was written for the 1914 war, but it has been sung year after year and has lost none of the urgency of its drama.

The *Three Carols* for chorus in unison and 'ad lib.' orchestra have also lasted through the years. Only those who have had to conduct 'drop-in-and-sing' festivals can know the joy of coming across a set of orchestral parts where the accompaniment still sounds completely satisfying even if an uninvited B♭ cornet turns up at the last rehearsal and the one available clarinet gets influenza on the day of the performance. Holst was a conductor who allowed all genuine amateurs to play in his orchestras 'if humanly possible'. One can imagine how they enjoyed themselves: there is an exuberance in the clanging discords of *On this Day* and in the vigorous delight with which he has 'cast a-down the proud' in *Masters in this Hall*.

In these days we take it for granted that our carols should dance, but in 1916 many of them were still either raucously plodding or mildly sentimental. Choirs must have welcomed the lively demands for a drink in *Bring us in good ale* and the memorable grace and freedom of *Lullay my liking*.

There is nothing for amateurs in the *Four Songs for voice and violin*: the extreme economy of the writing makes the most exacting demands on the singer and the player. It was an amateur, however, who had first given him the idea of writing the songs: he had gone into Thaxted church one evening and had heard a woman walking about in the empty aisles, improvising on her violin while singing a wordless song.

Jesu Sweet has the feeling of an improvisation, and both singer and player are as one: the few chords bind the recitative together, bringing an added intensity to the words. The opening of the second song has packed a lifetime of experience into its few notes:

Ex. 35.

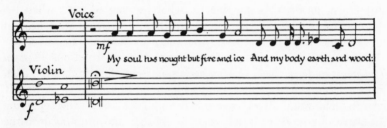

There is passion in the depth of the violin's E♭, and a sense of space in the voice's entry, as if the fifth had been waiting to sound within the held octave: the word 'fire' takes its warmth from the wide interval of the major sixth, and there is a radiance in the icy return to the fifth, the vowel blending with the strings' tone and the hissing sibilant adding to the steeliness. The E♮ of 'earth' knows the desperation of all the ills that flesh is heir to, as it pulls against the framework of the octave D before coming to rest on the unison.

I sing of a maiden has the same wealth of imagination: the violin's entry on a *pp* A¹ is quiet and unobtrusive enough to convey the stillness of the dew falling on the grass; when the dew falls on the spray, spreading out into a pattern like flowers on a bare twig, the violin spreads and flowers with it, holding up the pattern to the light with the clear outline of its chord of D.

Holst once referred to *My Leman is so true* as a good instance of a tune at one with the words—he felt that it was the nearest approach he had yet achieved in his search for the musical idiom of the English language. The violin's flowing counterpoint is inseparable from the rise and fall of the singer's phrase, and at the words 'I'll dwell with thee', he instinctively turns to the rhythm of the effortless dance that was his vision of heaven.

The same vision was to lead him, soon afterwards, to the fierce exaltation of *The Hymn of Jesus*.

CHAPTER VIII

THE HYMN OF JESUS AND
THE ODE TO DEATH

(1917-19)

WHEN *The Hymn of Jesus* was first performed the music came as a shock to those of the listeners who were not prepared to accept such astoundingly unfamiliar religious music. Holst had no use whatever for conventionality: he was utterly free from any routine piety, his memories of the B minor Mass were of ecstasy, his Sanskrit studies had taught him to think beyond the boundaries of Europe, and his idea of Christ included the terrifying unexpectedness of the Byzantine mosaics. It was only natural that he should disregard nineteenth-century oratorio as if it had never existed. Not that he breaks away from all tradition; *The Hymn of Jesus* is built on a foundation of plainsong, but instead of dwelling in a separate modal world the language is caught up and transformed in the excitement of his intensely imaginative mind. The impression the music leaves is of overwhelming religious exaltation. It is no good describing such an exaltation in words: it has to be sung or played or listened to. Analysis is bound to destroy the fervour, just as it is bound to destroy all sense of proportion when it stops the music in order to stare at its occasional moments of weakness.

Holst made his own translation of the hymn, with the help of one of his pupils. He knew very little Greek, but he copied out each word separately from the original apocryphal hymn, and then wrote down the pronunciation and the literal English equivalent. After that, as with the translations from the Sanskrit hymns, he pondered for a long time over the meaning of the words, and then made his own version to suit his own needs.

It is typical of him that before beginning work on the music, he should have taken the trouble to visit a monastery, to be quite sure he had got the right phrasing for the two plainsong hymns, 'Pange lingua' and 'Vexilla regis'. It is also typical that when giving the unaccompanied opening to the two tenor trombones in unison, he should carefully mark in directions for the position of each note, so as to avoid all danger of smearing. The ex-trombone player knew what could be done. There is, in this introduction, an unknowing recollection of the sound of medieval brass in a cathedral; when the first harmonies are heard they spread outwards with the gesture of a sixteenth-century motet. The flute quavers at the Lento carry their unhurried triads of G to and fro with a measured step that was first heard as long ago as in *The Mystic Trumpeter*: meeting the piercing F♯¹ of the oboe, English horn, and viola, they give a warning of what is to come. At the *senza misura* the organ's calm 'Vexilla regis' leads to those alternating chords that brought peace in *Venus*: the bare fourths and fifths move in and out with an aloof tranquillity, allowing the sopranos to chant their plainsong in freedom, until they are interrupted by the passionate outcry of the C major triad over F♯ and A♯:

Ex. 36.

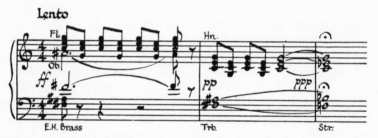

This sound holds within it the conflict of suffering that underlies the whole of the work: both chords must give way before they can melt into each other and lose their tension in the murmur of the 'Pange lingua'.

The sudden outburst on 'Glory to Thee, Father' moves dramatically from the bare C to the richness of the second inversion of E over a descending scale that links both keys, a scale he had already learnt in the *Choral Hymns from the Rig Veda*. Each line of the hymn is bound to the next by the floating rise and fall of the 'Amen' from the semi-chorus of sopranos and altos: heard on the piano, these parallel triads have a deceptive way of sounding like aimless drifting, but when they are sung they have a clear outline and purpose, for the sopranos are in A minor while the altos are in F minor. It is a figure that needs untempered singing. This also applies to the change of harmony when the octave C at 'Glory to Thee' moves to A♭ minor on 'Word': here the high A♭ of the sopranos and tenors is a startlingly different sound from their high G♯ on 'Father'. At 'Glory to Thee, O Grace' the *pp* chanting on an actual unison D♮ gives an extraordinary effect of a multitude of voices, owing to the mingled separateness of the low notes of the sopranos and the high notes of the basses. At the word 'Grace', when the music for the first time reaches the key of C, the sense of arrival is like a recognition.

The spoken 'Glory to Thee, Holy Spirit' was an experiment that failed to come off. But this may be because choirs rarely manage to get the right tone of voice. He meant it to be breathed almost in a whisper, with hardly any spoken pitch behind the vowels, but with tremendous energy in the clear consonants.

When the two choruses alternate between passive and active entreaty at 'Fain would I be saved' and 'Fain would I save', their balanced phrases are linked by the floating Amens of the semi-chorus. There is a moment of overwhelming intensity at the line 'Fain would I be pierced', where the smooth contrapuntal approach through C minor emerges on to the sudden pain of $D\flat_1 B_1 F E^1$ and is driven towards that other more poignant suffering of 'Fain would I pierce'.

The poco animato at 'Fain would I bear' is a dangerous turning-point; these short phrases in sequence have a way of sounding scrappy instead of accumulative. He was momentarily defeated by the technical problem of having to break up the sustained andante before going back to his alternating fourths and fifths for the calm conviction of 'I am Mind of all'.

In the dance that grows out of 'Fain would I be known' he reaches the fundamental idea of the hymn, the idea expressed in the words 'Ye who dance not, know not what we are knowing'. Its five-four allegro is so uncompromisingly insistent that critics have often complained of the 'vicarious' violence of all the repetition. But Holst needed the insistence of these wild leaps to match the exaltation of 'Divine Grace is dancing'. Throughout the hymn he keeps the shape of his music closely related to the vision of the words, as in the link between 'fain would I set in order' and 'the Heavenly Spheres make music for us', and between the moving outwards of the second chorus on 'fain would I be enfolded' and the moving inwards of the answering first chorus on 'fain would I enfold'. At 'I have Heaven' the dance continues through the Prelude's alternating chords, balancing the tranquillity of 'I am Mind of all', and leading to the sound that had been haunting him since he was a student, the dazzling sound of 'To you who gaze a lamp am I'. The voices are not burdened past their strength by the intensity of these discords: the passage is as singable as Palestrina, for the block counterpoint moves smoothly away from its unisons, leaving the long sustained notes in security. The sound and the vision approach very near to each other: for an instant the eye is dazzled by a light that is too bright to be gazed at; then gradually the lamp comes into focus as the mind is able to accept its illumination:

Ex. 37.

It is Holst's own way of expressing an unconscious memory of the most overwhelming mystical experience he had ever known in his life, when he had first heard the sustained radiance of:

Ex. 38.

The chordal counterpoint holds the same ecstasy at 'To you that know, a mirror': the lower level of the voices, the quieter singing, and the closer texture help to turn the radiance inwards at the word 'know', making the air quiver with the premonition of that later prolonged hush on 'wisdom'.

When the plainsong 'Give ye heed unto my dancing' reaches the crescendo at 'For yours is the passion of man that I go to endure', the alternating chords leave their aloof tranquillity, the bare fourths becoming augmented, and the fifths diminished. The suffering increases as the trumpets challenge each other with all the agony of the pursuit in *Mars*. Suddenly the bassoons break into their unforgettable twelve-eight 'Vexilla regis': the tune is lifted to the high, triumphant forte of the sopranos, whose chanted 'Ah' stretches out to the alternating chords, making them shed their anguish. The nightmare trumpet-call has also cast off its panic and is transformed into an Alleluia that joyfully accepts suffering and defeat as the banners advance.

But he was not able to keep up the intensity. At 'Beholding what I suffer' there is a conventional patch of commonplace sequences and calculated imitation, reaching its lowest abyss at 'Had ye known how to suffer, ye would know how to suffer no more', where he combines the sequences with a British Empire brand of descending bass in a fat, self-satisfied three-in-a-bar, while a *più mosso* guiltily tries to cover up the poverty of the musical thought. Many years afterwards a critic pointed out the shallowness of this passage, and he wished he could have rewritten it.

He recovers the lost mood of the hymn in the piercing notes of the high trumpet's 'Pange lingua' at 'Learn how to suffer and ye shall overcome'. There is a return to the dazzling radiance of Ex. 37 at 'Behold in me a couch', the chord of C at 'Rest on me' bringing back the same sense of recognition as at 'Glory to Thee, O Grace'. At 'Fain would I move to the music of holy souls' the leaping dance rhythm becomes flowing at last, as it moves quietly to the rising scale of 'the Heavenly Spheres make music for us'. The sound expands into the last of the dazzling phrases for 'Know in me the word of wisdom': the singers close their lips on the whole-tone murmur of the final 'm', making the air tremble with their vibrations. The sound is not an 'effect'; it grows inevitably from what has gone before, just as it sinks inevitably into the long silence that follows it, until the coda leads back to the burst of exaltation and the last floating Amens stretch upwards and come to rest.

The Hymn of Jesus was by far the best work he had yet written. The music is great enough to withstand occasional weaknesses when it is heard today. But it lacks the unity it might have had if he could have combined the mature skill of 1927 with the exuberance of 1917.

Some of the lessons of its weaknesses were still unlearnt when he wrote the *Ode to Death*, a setting for chorus and orchestra of the poem by Walt Whitman. These words reflected his own thought: the opening invitation, 'Come, lovely and soothing death', drew from him the serene sounds that belong to the mood of *Saturn*'s calm acceptance and of *Savitri*'s 'Welcome, Lord'. Nothing destroys the tranquillity of this opening; the harp's distant fifths thread their way through the held A of the murmured 'Come', and the hushed chord of B♭ branches into eight parts as it spreads through the divided chorus. The interchange of A major and B♭ minor at 'serenely arriving in the day, in the night' leads to the unaccompanied simplicity of:

Ex. 39.

But immediately the serenity is shattered by the impetuous rush of the B♭ minor arpeggio as it scrambles uphill to arrive on a fortissimo chord of D minor: the singers' 'Prais'd be the fathomless universe!' mounts from the repeated hammering of the D minor to a high A♭ on a pentatonic 'universe', with a gesture that lacks the confident strength of that other outburst on 'Glory to Thee, Word'.

The next passage is the weakest in the whole work: the trite entries on 'For life and joy' insist on thrusting themselves forward with a display of conventional imitation that knocks the harmonies into the eighteen-nineties: it is as if the influence of Whitman's poetry were driving him back to the days of his first apprenticeship.

The characteristic five-four ostinato with its pizzicato crotchets and sustained trombones was inevitable for the mood of 'when thou must indeed come, come unfalteringly'. The quietly drifting parallel semitones of 'Lost in the lovely floating ocean' possess a quality that is only to be found in the *Ode to Death*, when Holst was mid-way between the harmonic chromaticism of his pre-1914 days and the contrapuntal chromaticism of the prelude to the *Choral Symphony*. But the tenderness is soon pushed aside by the four-square determination of 'From me to thee glad serenades', where the staccato off-the-beat dominant-to-tonic of the trumpets and trombones betrays a forced attempt to make the words sound exhilarating. It is a relief

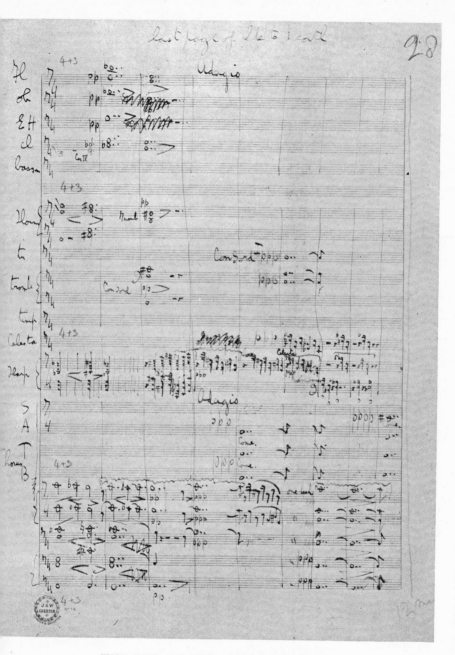

THE END OF THE *ODE TO DEATH*

to return to the peace of the opening fifths and to be led to a sentence in Holst's unmistakable voice:

Ex. 40.

It is in these unaccompanied passages that his imagination is secure: the limitations of the dependent threads of counterpoint help to keep his harmonies from wandering off the track he is trying to follow. The bare fourths hold all that he needs for 'the body gratefully nestling close to thee'; the rising phrase speaks the language of 'Fain would I be enfolded'.

When the sopranos sing 'Over the tree-tops I float thee a song' their tune floats with effortless grace over the quietly repeated chords of the harp. There is only one instant where the freely exploring tonality is jerked to a stand-still by the insistence of those defining harmonies: it is when the rising scale of F♯ minor sails up to its E♯ and hovers there, before changing to F♮ for 'I float'. Sung unaccompanied, this phrase is full of possibilities, but it is weakened by the obvious modulation.

The weakness is soon blotted out at the return to the opening mood of calm acceptance. This is the mood that remains in the listening mind, and it is owing to this mood that the *Ode to Death* still lives. There is the very essence of Holst's thought in that final pause on the word 'Come', where the sound, dissolving into silence, removes the last barrier between supplication and surrender.

F

CHAPTER IX

THE PERFECT FOOL

(1918–22)

HOLST was in the Middle East from the autumn of 1918 to the summer of 1919, organizing music for the troops who were waiting to be demobilized. It was a busy life, and it gave him very little chance for composing, but on his journeys between teaching sight-singing and conducting festivals of English music he managed to think of the outlines of his opera, *The Perfect Fool*.

It was twenty-five years since his last attempt at a comic opera had been laboriously rehearsed and irrevocably abandoned in a basement room at the Royal College of Music. During those twenty-five years he had learnt a great deal, but he had not yet learnt that he was incapable of writing his own libretto. *The Perfect Fool* taught him this lesson, though not until after it had been produced at Covent Garden.

The opera begins with a ballet, adapted from an earlier work called *The Sneezing Charm*. It is danced by the Spirits of Earth, Water, and Fire. The Wizard, a direct descendant of *Uranus* and *Phantastes*, summons the Spirits of the Earth with a trombone invocation that rises in angular fury and descends in marcato whole-tone deliberation, and orders them to bring him a cup for working magic. The quavers of the ostinato bass travel persistently between C and F♯; staccato triads hop over them, intent on the same journey, and semiquavers run uphill, beginning in C and landing on F♯, strengthening the ties of a relationship that was already close and inescapable in his own mind. When the dance begins the clumsy, clodhopping seven-eight remains intentionally earth-bound, but the weight of the syncopation is balanced and the tune has none of the distended awkwardness of Ex. 29. From the lowest depths of the orchestra, the energetic huskiness of the double-basses over the quietly ponderous tonguing of the double bassoon conjures up an appropriate earthiness. The consecutive fourths that clatter their way up and down the three-eight tune were also intended to be appropriate, but their haggard liveliness suggests that they were in danger of hardening into a formula. When the Earth Spirits have reached the climax of their dance, to the leaping cross-rhythm of the seven-eight over the three-eight ostinato, they scurry underground on one of Holst's favourite

mixed scales, leaving the solo viola to call up the Spirits of the Water
with a legato rising phrase on the C string, which can hardly be
recognized as the same five notes of the trombones' invocation, so far
is it removed from all trace of jagged ill-temper.

The cool wood-wind chords and the dripping fifths of the harp and
celesta lead to the second dance, where, with the help of the flute,
the Spirits of the Water bring 'the essence of love distilled from
Aether'. This magic potion is concocted according to Holst's own
recipe, not one drop of sweetness being allowed to cling to the sides
of the cup.

When the Wizard invokes the Spirits of Fire the dance crackles
into a sudden spurt and approaches inch by inch, the staccato fifths
of the bassoons sounding as brittle as burning stubble. Like the earth
dance, it is founded on ostinato quavers in the bass with sudden
changes from C to Db or C to B, while the time-pattern acquires its
self-assertion by saying the same thing over and over again. Considered dispassionately, there is far too much reliance on repetition
in this ballet, and far too much similarity in the construction of the
tunes. The same habit of speech can be heard in the rising scuffle in
the earth dance:

Ex. 41.

and in the cool legato of the Spirits of the Water:

Ex. 42.

and in the energetic blaze of the fire dance:

Ex. 43.

This is not an example of the economic use of his material, for there is no organic connexion between the three fragments. He was obviously unable to prevent several of his mannerisms from threatening to destroy the vitality of the dances: there are moments when the music sounds as if he were parodying himself. The same mannerisms recur soon afterwards in a short ballet called *The Lure*, where it is impossible to ignore the fact that he was repeating himself and relying on his brilliant orchestration to make the music sound exciting.

When *The Perfect Fool* ballet comes to an end the listener is immediately aware of the painful inadequacy of Holst's libretto. The Wizard's first spoken remark, 'But I am weary', comes as a shock, owing to its conversational tone of voice: when he sits down and leans back, with an audible sigh of satisfaction that is half-yawn and half-grunt, one is plunged into the uncomfortable sensation of having been tricked into attending the performance of a charade instead of an opera. And all the time the music says everything that needs to be said: there is genuine humour in the bassoons' hesitating unrelated staccato triads as they imitate the cautious gestures of a garrulous old imposter settling down to sleep. The Mother's voice is heard in the distance: she comes in dragging the Fool after her, complaining that she is homeless and hungry, her melancholy five-four leaning on its characteristic augmented second. She quotes the prophecy about her half-witted son: 'He wins a bride with a glance of his eye: with a look he kills a foe. He achieves where others fail, with one word.' She tries to wake him up, but he only yawns and goes to sleep again. Her conversation with the Wizard is embarrassingly amateurish, the spoken dialogue sounding exactly like a middle-school play on the last night of term. He tells her that he is going to drink the magic potion as soon as the Princess comes along, because there is an ancient prophecy that runs: 'She shall marry the man who does the deed no other can do.' The Wizard's galumphing dance has the purposeful clumsiness of *Uranus* in its twisted, burlesque folk-tune, as he boasts, 'I'll fulfil the prophecy, I shall win the bride'. His rehearsal of the wooing song is superbly appropriate in its ridiculous emphasis:

Ex. 44.

Moderato

f Queen of this land and all our hearts, O Queen of love-li-ness,

The words 'fit' the five-four rhythm but fall headlong into absurd traps of false declamation. Suddenly the tune breaks off for his spoken injunction: 'Now listen attentively: I'm coming to the important part.' It is these conversational remarks that make the opera unendurable. The Wizard's spoken exclamation: 'You're the worst actress I've ever met—no feeling, no imagination, no sense of style!' is so devastatingly life-like that it sounds just as if Holst were sitting over a meal and exchanging comic anecdotes with one of his friends. It has caught the unmistakable inflection of his tone of voice, but it is disastrous in a libretto.

When the Wizard has fallen asleep again there is a rare moment of lyrical beauty as three girls come in and fill their pitchers at the well, singing a round in praise of water. By the time the Mother has managed to pour the magic potion down the Fool's throat (needless to say he chokes) and has filled the empty cup with clear water, the atmosphere increasingly resembles a pageant for amateurs: the entry of the Princess to a fanfare of trumpets with the chorus of attendants talking in groups is straight out of a Morley College bank-holiday celebration. The arrival of the Verdi Troubadour is a welcome relief, for he brings flowing continuity to the music. His song is only a parody, but it seems surprisingly real in the middle of all the ingenious cross-rhythms, while his emotion, intended to be fictitious, has a disconcerting way of sounding genuine after so many brittle fourths. He woos deliciously in six-eight over the correct harmonic background, with the right grace-notes in the first verse and the right chromatic passing-notes in the second, and his competition with the Princess for the top notes in the cadenza is graceful and unforced. The Wagnerian Traveller is also welcome, and the comedy reaches its highest level when the Princess refuses his proposal with the words: 'But, Sir, I think we have heard this before', to the tune of Siegfried's horn-call. Holst must have got an enormous amount of enjoyment out of writing the Traveller's protesting sequences on 'Nay, O Nay, Noisiest Negative', followed by the stage direction that the rest of the outburst is to be drowned by the orchestra.

When the Traveller gesticulates too excitedly and stumbles over the Fool, the Fool wakes up and looks at the Princess and the spell works, making the Princess fall in love with him in the right fairy-tale manner.

To the trickling murmur of the ballet music she moves towards him as if in a trance, quoting the flute's slow dance tune as she tells him how she has waited for him. This is Holst's own way of writing a

love-song: aloof, impersonal, and in another world. When the Fool
yawns in her face and the Mother tries to prevent him falling asleep
again, she sings 'No! Do not wake him', with the pure, contemplative
ecstasy of a Titania enamoured of an ass. The situation is neither
comic nor pathetic: it would be impossible to laugh at her, for she has
entered an enchanted region where mortal discrepancies have ceased
to matter; to sympathize with her would be presumptuous.

Comedy returns with the gesticulatory diminished sevenths of the
Troubadour's recitative, his cadential six-four being snatched from
under his feet by the Traveller's chromatic outcry of 'Revenge!' The
Verdi retainers are directed to become 'conventionally agitated' while
singing 'She shall be thine' on repeated semiquavers, until they also
are interrupted by the Traveller, whose 'Vaulting vengeance my
bosom burneth' grows uncomfortably higher at each sequence as he
passionately endeavours to compete with the ever-thickening brass
of his own over-weighted accompaniment.

When the shepherd brings the message that a forest fire is spreading
it becomes obvious that Holst had still got a good deal to learn about
stage timing. There is urgency in the message, and yet he wants to
convey the shepherd's pastoral background; the series of quietly
flowing first inversions on the horns is a lovely sound, but it is local
atmosphere applied unthinkingly, and it damages the dramatic unfolding of the story. With the growing excitement of defence preparations
and the enlistment of fire-fighters the thing once more becomes a
charade: there is a terrifically exciting noise when the eight trumpeters
—four on the stage and four in the orchestra—are encouraged to
improvise their own *ad lib.* variations on their fanfare.

While the chorus is getting into line Holst skilfully combines the
two contrasting moods of the scene; the tenors and basses are still
muttering 'Sound the call for battle' in their staccato six-eight when
the Princess lifts her andante flute tune high over their heads,
singing, 'While we fret and struggle, while we toil and strive, Great
Ones, cloth'd in wisdom, watch from thrones of peace.' It is the
language of *Savitri* and of the hymns from the *Rig Veda*: in this
meeting-place the two worlds can exist side by side. It no longer
matters that the Princess has been bewitched and that it is just by
accident she is in a state of grace: she has found the only real security.

When the Wizard comes in surrounded by his Spirits of Fire,
everyone rushes out leaving the Mother, the Fool, and the Princess
alone on the stage. The Fool turns his magic gaze on the Wizard and
shrivels him up; the fire dies down. Members of the chorus creep back

on tip-toe, a few at a time, 'looking round anxiously' as the stage direction says. But, as it happens, they creep back in genuine panic, looking anxiously at the conductor, for Holst has brought them in on an unaccompanied four-part fugue beginning:

Ex. 45.

The agony of waiting through the rests before trying to place those naked, unsympathetic intervals is written all too plainly on their faces: consciously or unconsciously, the fugue becomes a parody of all the apprehensive entries of the chorus that have ever driven their producers frantic at rehearsals.

The Princess, having upbraided them for deserting her, turns to the Fool and asks him if he loves her. He has sunk into a coma of apathy and she has to ask him the same question three times. At last, after she has paused inquiringly on her high D, he makes a supreme effort and comes out with his only word in the opera, the word 'No'. But Holst's judgement of orchestration failed him for once: the richness of that highly spiced discord on wood-wind and horns is too overpowering for an accompaniment to the spoken voice, and the hero's one word is in danger of getting lost.

There is a return to the mood of a bank-holiday pageant when the chorus turns on the Fool in a fury and the Mother reminds the Princess that 'he has achieved where others failed, with one word—for he is the only man who has ever looked in your face and not loved you'.

General rejoicing, ending in a moment of anticlimax at the curtain, when the Fool yawns a luxuriously long-drawn-out yawn and falls asleep again just as he is about to be crowned.

Bewildered audiences found this anticlimax the last straw. They complained, with some justification, that even when the·curtain had fallen they had not yet discovered what the story had been about. Many different theories were brought forward, including Tovey's ingenious suggestion that the Princess was meant to represent 'Opera', while the Fool was 'The British Public'. There were no theories in Holst's mind: as usual, he wrote exactly what he wanted to say. He had no idea that the opera would prove to be puzzling or embarrassing, just as he had no idea that he was getting into the habit of writing too many consecutive fourths. He was still too near to the work and too closely involved in the excitement of its production to be conscious of a feeling of unreality in some of the music. But perhaps unconsciously he may have felt that he needed to escape from the slavery of those all-too-easy consecutives into the freedom that could be found in the inexorable limitations of counterpoint.

CHAPTER X

NEO-CLASSICISM AND THE CHORAL SYMPHONY
(1922–4)

'Tomorrow I may do something quite different', Holst once wrote
to a friend. He had been discussing his aversion to fixed principles in
art, and had quoted his favourite piece of advice: 'Never compose
anything unless the not composing of it becomes a positive nuisance
to you.'

The 'something quite different' in 1922 was the *Fugal Overture*
for orchestra. One has to take his word for it that he found it a
nuisance not to write this work, for it gives the impression that he
had deliberately set out to write an intellectual exercise. He had never
heard of neo-classicism: Stravinsky had not yet written his Octet
for Wind, nor had Hindemith begun work on his Kammermusik
Op. 36. If Holst's *Fugal Overture* seems to coincide with the beginnings of the miscalled 'back-to-Bach' movement, it is not because
he had allowed himself to be drawn into following a new fashion,
but because his own inquiring mind had led him up that particular
path at that particular moment.

He had meant to write a fugal ballet, but by the time he had finished
it he decided it would do as an overture to *The Perfect Fool*, if one
should be needed. In the opening bars the ear is assaulted by the
blatancy of the repeated pentatonic chord on full wood-wind and
brass as it hammers out the time-pattern of Ex. 46. This fugal subject
bristles with angular cross-rhythms:

Ex. 46.

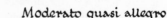

Under the cerebral spikes of its accents lurks the hint of a lively
dance:

Ex. 47.

But it seldom has a chance of sounding like that, for the false entries in close stretto frown on all attempts at abandon. When the trombones come in on a *ff* second subject, cutting across the four-four with an implied five-eight time-pattern that is utterly at variance with the first subject's cross-rhythms, the music resembles a cleverly worked-out mathematical problem. After a *fff* repetition which is in no sense a climax, since there is no growth of intensity other than the mechanical increase in dynamics, it is a merciful deliverance to be brought to the quiet augmentation, where the strings are given the first half of the subject in pizzicato crotchets. The mood here is reminiscent of the anxious entry of the chorus in *The Perfect Fool*, when the question 'where is the fire?' is muttered in a staccato sotto voce. A later Holst emerges at the meno mosso, when the cello's improvisation leads to the remote solitude of the world of *Egdon Heath*:

Ex.48.

But this oasis is soon left behind. There is an inescapable return to the fugue, enlivened for an instant by the comic dialogue between the piccolo and the double bassoon, and then the noise begins all over again. Unsatisfactory as the work is, it had its uses, not only as a lesson in counterpoint, but also as a rehearsal for other works where he had got something more important to say and had learnt to say it without such over-insistence.

The *Fugal Concerto* for flute, oboe, and string orchestra was the first thing he wrote after his recovery from an accident in February 1923, when he had slipped from a rostrum while conducting and had fallen on the back of his head. The concerto has a dry and brittle ingenuity in its counterpoint which has led many people to suppose that concussion was responsible for banishing him into what they call the 'arid desert' of his later works. But he had already begun exploring these contrapuntal labyrinths at least half a year before his accident, and the punctilious formality of the *Fugal Concerto* is gracious compared with the calculated violence of the *Fugal Overture*. Whatever effect the concussion may have had on his writing, it was certainly not to be blamed for starting him off on the track of neo-classicism.

In the first movement of the *Concerto* the fugue is carried out in traditional eighteenth-century style, the voices entering at the expected keys and the modulations working according to approved patterns. The subject appears inverted and in stretto: episodes are founded on it, and there is the usual dominant pedal note. Through all these decorous gestures of a borrowed courtesy it is possible to recognize his usual tone of voice in the pesante quavers that sound like good-natured but compulsory slow practice, and in the delicate, almost pedantic humour of the last *pp* entry. The slow movement has a flowing tune whose melancholy wandering remains diatonic. A pizzicato descending scale walks deliberately over the three-four bar-line and takes its own leisurely three-two time, as in the Inter-mezzo of the *St. Paul's Suite*. The turn of the phrase between the second and third bar of the subject blossoms into a lyrical episode, and there is a moment of ravishing beauty when the oboe thrusts upwards through the first five notes of the scale of A, arriving and pausing on its E while the violins are still breathing their quiet repeated E♯ and G♯ from the triad of C♯ major. There is nothing in the least 'modern' about this exquisite sound: it belongs to the same world as the slow movement of the first Brandenburg concerto, where the cellos stretch upwards to their passing A♭ at the same instant that the violins decide to lean downwards on to their pass-ing A♮.

The tune in the last movement is yet another example of Holst's habit of saying the same thing three times with a different implication at each change of stress:

Ex.49.

The habit refused to be shaken off, and had long since become instinctive. But the listener finds it difficult to avoid the suspicion that the change of emphasis has been carefully worked out on paper.

If Holst had not marked in the accents this suspicion might not loom so large; the tune can skip along quite happily if it is left to find its own way. The counter-subject, founded on the first three notes of the inverted subject, brings with it an entirely new set of cross-accents, owing to the fact that it delays its entry for a couple of quavers. Later on we get the subject in augmentation at a pesante two-four against the original subject in close stretto and, by introducing the traditional dance tune 'If all the world were paper', he turns the movement into a double fugue. The venture can hardly be described as a happy marriage: for some reason the third and sixth quavers of the staccato subject refuse to blend with the smooth, lilting quavers of the dance. It is not that it ever sounds clumsy: the whole movement is neat and precise and highly polished. But it is the counterpoint of a skilful brain rather than of an exuberant spirit. On the whole it is just as well he never tried to repeat this particular experiment.

That same year he began work on the *Choral Symphony*. While writing it he led what he called 'the life of a real composer'. He had been overworking for so long that at last he had been compelled to give up teaching for a whole year. He lived by himself in the country and was able to compose every day of the week, instead of having to save up his ideas for Sundays. The change was not altogether a success for he had never learnt to take things easily, and it is possible that many of the failings of the *Choral Symphony* were due to the difficulty of adjusting himself to his compulsory leisure. The work contains some of the finest music he had yet written, but it suffers from his inability to write in extended form. The slow movement and the Scherzo are satisfying in themselves, but in the first movement and the Finale he was defeated by the problem of trying to develop his ideas to the required length and breadth of a symphony. He would have been far happier if he had decided to write several shorter movements which could have been strung together with something of the continuity of an eighteenth-century secular cantata. But he felt it was necessary to grapple with the difficulties of writing in symphonic form.

He chose his selection of poems by Keats with complete disregard for all orthodox literary judgement, sandwiching the 'Ode on a Grecian Urn' between some of the verses Keats tossed off in his letters to his friends and his family. The mixture is startling, and has caused the brows of purists to darken with disapproval. But Holst was obstinate, insisting that he knew what he wanted for his particular purpose.

The Prelude is an invocation to Pan. There is a low persistent murmur of an octave B, stretching down below the double-basses' normal compass; gradually the muted strings unfold their melancholy fugue while the altos and basses mutter their 'eternal whispers . . . in heavy peacefulness'. The chromatic counter-subject rises from the depths; its drifting semitones are as insubstantial as a wraith of mist, yet they alter the contours of the music as they float past:

Ex.50.

It is one of those landscapes of the mind where Holst's thought moves most freely.

At the beginning of the Song the viola's *senza misura* draws out the rising melodic fourths that recur throughout the whole symphony. The sadness of the Phrygian tune is intensified by the dying fall at the end of each line as the solo soprano keeps 'brimming the

water-lily cups with tears'. And then suddenly the revellers interrupt
her solitary weeping and burst into their dance:

Ex. 51.

Allegretto

This Bacchanal has been described as 'exciting in its pagan orgy of
sound'. There is certainly a good deal of excitement in the orchestration, with its crisp staccato wood-wind and its *col legno* strings and
its jingles and xylophone. And if 'pagan' means repeating the same
primitive time-pattern over and over again then it is also pagan. But
with the best will in the world it cannot be called intoxicating. One
longs for a suggestion of mellow warmth, that the magic of the
wine may be allowed to flow through all the listening veins. These
highly strung revellers, 'all madly dancing' with 'faces all on flame',
seem able to keep up their energetic seven-eight on nothing stronger
than soda-water: their consecutive fourths are too persistently perfect
to have been allowed to ferment. It is difficult to avoid casting a
backward glance of regret at the immature *Hymn to Dionysus*, where
the music was not afraid of sounding sensuous. But it is useless to
complain: if Holst wanted his own version of austerity bacchanalia
in 1924 he was entitled to it.

When the tempo of the music slows down for the tenors and basses
to ask: 'Whence came ye, merry Damsels?' the 'new' tune turns out
to be built up on descending melodic fourths, as perfect as ever,
with pesante horns still obstinately supplying consecutive perfect
fourths beneath them. The habit had become a menace, and was
threatening to undermine the whole structure of the movement.

The bustle of the Bacchanal is immediately forgotten in the cool
and tranquil world of the *Ode on a Grecian Urn*. The slowly rising
fifths might seem at first to be returning to the hushed mood of the
Prelude, but a pencilled note in Holst's writing says: 'Not mysterious,
but clear-cut, like sunshine on frost.' This was the clarity of vision
that was peculiarly his own. He was able to look from an immense

distance at the frozen sunlight of those leaf-fringed forests in Arcady and to note, with careful attention to detail, the attitude and expression of each of those marble men and maidens. He could translate the stillness of their movements into music that flows almost imperceptibly.

The muted fifths rise from the bare outline of the open strings; the gathered sounds float on the frosty air and call forth an answer from the three flutes, whose characteristic quaver triads wave to and fro between G♯ minor and A minor. The entry of the singers is so quiet that their octave E blends with the muted held fifths and can scarcely be heard until it rises and spreads to the second inversion of G♯ minor for the word 'quietness'. There is real enchantment here: the hush of the cellos' and bassoons' low C♮ and G♮ beneath this chord of G♯ minor is quieter than any other moment in the symphony, and the concentrated indifference of the rhythm of 'silence and slow time' has the same static quality as *Neptune*.

The unaccompanied chant at 'Sylvan historian', which is quoted for the last two lines of every verse in the Ode, binds the pattern of the music with its sad symmetry. At the 'pipes and timbrels' the open fifths become resonant with overtones ás the clash sets the whole air vibrating, and the quivering flood of sound is intensified at the long pause on the word 'ecstasy', where the voices are left holding the second inversion of the dominant seventh of G under the second inversion of E♭.

There is a return to the bare frostiness at 'Heard melodies are sweet'. Was this perhaps one of the passages which made listeners complain of the 'arid wastes' of the symphony? There is certainly not an ounce of sweetness to be squeezed out of these four words. But Holst's mind had enveloped the whole sentence: he was already carried into the mood of 'not to the sensual ear, but . . . to the spirit'. The sad descending whole-tone scale is exactly suited to the 'ditties of no tone', especially when the unaccompanied voices of the tenors sink to their lower register. The ear waits for the 'soft pipes' to play on, and when the flutes quote their waving triads the sound is welcomed as inevitable. These same unhurried quavers are woven into the music of 'Ah, happy, happy boughs', bringing to it the non-rigid stillness that belongs to the later *Betelgeuse*, where 'time is a bird whose wings have never stirred the golden avenues of leaves'.

The aloofness relents at 'for ever panting and for ever young', when the pause holds out its earlier 'ecstasy' in contrast to the severe depths of 'all breathing human passion far above'. At this point the

spoken words could not convey what the music has to express as
it steps beyond the dimensional barriers of time, prolonging the
quivering discord of 'young' and filling the emptiness of those unlived
centuries, so that the altos and basses reach the tranquillity of all
passion spent with youth still pulsating in their ears.

As the sound dies away the altos draw the verse to an end with
their reminder that human passion 'leaves a heart high-sorrowful and
cloy'd, A burning forehead, and a parching tongue'. There is unerring
instinct in his choice of tone-colour for these final unadorned sentences: only the basses could have suggested the sympathetic but
unsatisfactory comfort in the assurance that 'she cannot fade, though
thou hast not thy bliss'. And here it is only the altos, in the fullness
of the most resonant notes of their compass, who can suggest the
cloying and the burning and the parching.

Several critics have felt that it was a mistake for Holst to lead
straight into the procession at 'Who are these coming to the sacrifice?'
without preparing in some way for the complete change of scene.
But the abrupt transition is implied in the poem: Keats has let his
gaze wander from those happy boughs and that happy melodist and
the still happier lover, remembering his own burning forehead and
his own parching tongue. Nothing is likely to distract him from his
present agony, unless he catches sight of those other remote figures
who are moving out of sight as their procession winds its way round
the unexplored surface of the Urn. His attention is held instantane-
ously, and Holst follows his glance, being alert at all times and being
fundamentally incapable of providing padding in his music.

The procession moves over a ground bass of pizzicato crotchets.
It is a leisurely progress they make through the quiet morning sunlight, the unhurried rhythm of the spoken words moulding the smooth
rise and fall of the tune. The chorus lifts its 'Fair attitude!' and the
open fifths expand until they are woven in and out for the 'forest
branches and the trodden weed', the interlacing triads drawing closer
and closer as they ruffle the clear-cut outlines of each twig and leaf.

And then, for the first time, the mood is shattered. At the return
to the processional tune for 'When old age shall this generation waste'
the ground bass leaves its tenacious purpose and begins to modulate
at each second bar, dragging the harmonies from their wonted austerity. This passage obviously gave him a good deal of trouble. In his
original version the ground remains constant and there are no
manœuvring semiquavers. It is not often that his revision shows less
economy than his first attempt: the lapse may have been one of the

penalties he was paying for the privilege of 'leading the life of a real composer'.

The rejected first sketches of the end of the movement show how his mind was groping for a perfection that eluded him. The words 'Beauty is truth' meant so much to him; he must have found it an overwhelmingly difficult task to have to disclose the very core of his belief. The music fails to express his certainty, and gets no farther than attempting to provide an adequate covering for the words. The triad of B minor over the held C♮ seems strangely disappointing: it is not that there is anything wrong with this very lovely sound in itself, but heard in this context it lacks the magic of the earlier 'quietness' and 'slow time'. The magic returns in the last few bars when the soprano becomes reconciled to the solitary lament of the first movement in the falling whole-tone phrase of 'all ye need to know'.

In the Scherzo, from the very first instant, the scene is set for the winged flight of a messenger as swift and uncircumscribed as *Mercury*. The muted strings' staccato scales fluctuate from one key to another, the peak of each flight being picked out with delicate precision by the wood-wind. The first entry of the voices looks alarmingly unsingable:

Ex. 52.

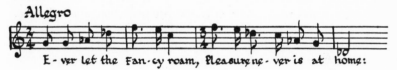

It is a challenge to the most experienced of choral societies, but the angularities soon sort themselves out into the familiar alternation between the chords of C and D♭. The sounds scatter, light as air, to let the 'wingéd Fancy wander Through the thought still spread beyond her'. The imagination behind every note can be felt in the subtle rhythm of the words and in the texture of their harmonies, as staccato wood-wind and pizzicato strings convey the intangible loss of 'At a touch sweet Pleasure melteth, Like to bubbles when rain pelteth'. When it comes to 'Open wide the mind's cage door, She'll dart forth and cloudward soar', the music whisks the words into a fluttering struggle to escape through the glitter of F minor and G♯ minor over a held C and G. Fancy's wings are equal to the struggle, and she emerges triumphantly on to a triad of C, the first brief resting-place in the movement. It is only for an instant: the fluttering contrapuntal interchange between C major and C♯ minor soon brings a reminder that 'the enjoying of the spring Fades as does its blossoming'. The ostinato is typical:

Ex. 53.

The leggiero octaves of the oboes and bassoons bring with them a suggestion of a crackle when 'the sear faggot blazes bright', and the held E on muted violins and double-basses lends a faint frostiness to the winter's night, leading to the magic of:

Ex. 54.

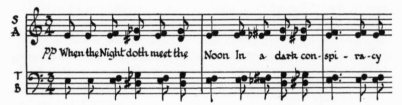

At the augmentation the rare word 'dolce' smoothes away the fluttering quavers and lends warmth to the promise that 'She will bring, in spite of frost, Beauties that the earth hath lost'. The quick patter begins again, leaving the brittle excitement of bitonality for a chattering modal tune that is tossed from one voice to another. There is a new enchantment in every line: no sooner have the sopranos sung 'Hark! 'Tis the early April lark', than the basses begin describing 'the rooks, with busy caw, Foraging for sticks and straw', their voices transformed by their brief encounter with the staccato quavers of the bass clarinet and the horns. These changes of colour are rapid, but they never interfere with the dancing continuity of the music; the lull of the legato augmentation as 'the hen-bird's wing doth rest Quiet on her mossy nest', is easily swept back into the light-hearted leggiero.

The middle section of the Scherzo, to the words of Folly's Song, is built on a cumbersome ground bass:

Ex. 55.

Holst first thought of this as one bar of nine-eight. It would perhaps have been better if he had kept to his original intention, for it needs the lift of a dance, and the persistent over-emphasis of the third note becomes as tiresome as those unnecessary accents in the last movement of the *Fugal Concerto*.

The tune that is sung to this ostinato also suffers from over-insistence: it belongs to the world of *Phantastes* and has borrowed the galumphing gait of one of those obstinate Wizards. It works up to a climax, getting quicker and louder as 'the barrel's set abroach', and the fifths in the ground bass lose their symmetry, arriving with a drunken list. When the reverberations of the loudest of all the crashes have sorted themselves out into scurrying quavers they bring the return of the Scherzo, played as an orchestral section without the chorus. The scintillating quavers of 'Open wide the mind's cage door' are at first distorted by the uproar of Folly's Song. Wood-wind and strings rattle through their fortissimo, while horns and trumpets bellow after them in augmentation. The trombones, determined not to be out-done, make several attempts at the presto quavers, before joining in a heavy-footed parody of 'Ever let the Fancy roam', thereby solving the problem of getting back to the first half of the Scherzo while the clamour of Folly's brawl is still filling the air. The outburst sobers the brass. The music quietens and becomes leggiero. Fragments of remembered tunes are scattered over the orchestra. Oboe, English horn, and bassoon quote the remark about the winter's night; a solitary piccolo recalls the early April lark. Both tunes combine, bringing the miracle that Fancy has promised, as they mix their pleasures of winter and summer. Clarinets draw down their dolce sixths for the wing that is quietly at rest; muted trumpet and trombone hop lightly over the surface of 'Oh sweet Fancy, let her loose!' inviting the strings to flutter their way through the prestissimo coda. Here the shifting sounds are light as gossamer: the violins escape and soar up to their triad of C; the piccolo breaks off in the middle of a whisper; the harp descends in a rapid glissando to finish the phrase in its lowest octave. There is a long pause as the muted horns hold their triad of D♭ minor against the violin's high chord of C; for the last time the web of enchantment is spread through the listening air. Then the double-basses gently snap the final thread with their pizzicato low E.

The Finale is the longest and the least satisfactory movement in the symphony. It reaches moments of true greatness, but they are isolated moments and they are unable to redeem the fundamental weakness of the form. The soprano sings the opening verse of 'Spirit here that reignest' in an unaccompanied *senza misura*; the full chorus and brass enter majestically at 'God of the golden bow', their melodic fourths piling up into chords, while each rising phrase grows in intensity. It is a magnificent sound, conveying Holst's high serious-ness of purpose, but there is no disguising the fact that we have already had an unconscionable number of these hard-worked intervals during the last twenty-five minutes. It seems a welcome change when the music forms into a procession and we are promised one of those hymn-like marches he so often wrote for his amateurs. The relief, however, turns to dismay as the hymn unfolds its harmonies and displays symptoms of a nobilmente nature. It is one of the few passages in the *Choral Symphony* which sounds irrevocably dated. Homer's twanging harp helps to draw the music back into its native element of fourths and fifths, but the nobilmente march insists on being heard again, the solemn expression of the horns and trombones making its platitudes sound even more embarrassing. The brass is also responsible for the unnecessary waiting about in the five bars before the entry of Shakespeare. Holst must have had his doubts about it for there are rough sketches of his attempts to come to a decision: he had already arrived on a unison E at the word 'peace', and it is difficult to guess why he should have tried to fill up a gap that need never have existed. It is one of the many weak patches where the unsatisfactory form interferes with the purpose of the movement.

When the Passions 'quickly forward spring', their leaping fourths fail to get them anywhere. As in the Bacchanal they are too con-sistently perfect to be passionate. But these same bare fourths are inevitable for 'the dying tones that fill the air' as they float in and out of their quietly moving five-four. The basses' pianissimo 'Bards of Passion' is scarcely recognizable as the offending march for the tune has been stripped of its nobilmente harmonies: violins and cellos hold a bare fourth while the violas and divisi double-basses lend their dark solemnity to the voices. At the 'whisper of heaven's trees' an espressivo steals through the music, the sounds becoming more and more impressionistic as the sopranos sing about the flowers. The mood is not very convincing, but perhaps the words are partly to blame, for no one would ask daisies to be 'rose-scented'. Holst himself felt slightly uncomfortable in this passage, and changed several harmonies which he considered 'too mild and luscious' for his taste. All traces of mildness disappear at 'heaven and its mysteries', and the movement ends in untroubled serenity, the chimes of 'Thus ye teach us' bringing an echo of the long-held 'wisdom' in *The Hymn of Jesus*.

While he was working at the symphony, Holst had thought it 'at least as good as, if not better than' anything he had written so far. It reaches heights that touch his greatest level, but it is frequently dragged down by its weaknesses, and owing to its lack of form it remains hovering in a half-comprehended void.

Some of the weaknesses are never heard again in any of his later works: the nobilmente maestoso has been played for the last time; the platitudinous sequences that marred *The Hymn of Jesus* and the *Ode to Death* will not lead him astray any more. There were to be other failures and other mistakes. And he had not yet discovered that he had still got to be on his guard against the mannerisms of the too-easy fourths and fifths. But never again was he to borrow the tatters of an applied romanticism.

He had another ten years left for the lessons that were still to be learnt.

CHAPTER XI

AT THE BOAR'S HEAD

(1924)

As it happened, the next work he wrote was condemned by nearly everyone who heard it. *At the Boar's Head* is a brilliant failure. He called it 'a musical interlude in one act', taking the words from the tavern scenes in Henry IV and fitting them to traditional morris and country-dance tunes and folk-songs. As soon as he had begun work on it he found, to his delight, that it was 'an opera that wrote itself', and he revelled in solving its intricate problems.

It was certainly a perilous undertaking. The words already conveyed everything that was needed in this richest of comedies, and the unaccompanied tunes were already complete in themselves. Bringing them together and trying to persuade them that they were meant for each other was a task which might have daunted anyone less obstinate than Holst. But he was not even aware of anything improbable in the mixture. Having discovered quite by chance that one of the morris tunes in Cecil Sharp's collection happened to 'fit' a sentence in the play he was reading, he set out to enjoy himself, indulging in his love of counterpoint and basking in the sense of freedom that it brought him.

Each syllable of the text is dealt with faithfully, and there are seldom any signs of strain in the writing. The counterpoint is effortless, seeming to happen quite casually and almost by accident. The joins between the folk-tunes are skilfully manœuvred: by repeatedly quoting short phrases that are shared by several of the tunes he manages to make each dance move on to the next with the utmost ease. He was no longer in the least troubled by having to get from one key to another: each change sounds inevitable. And he was no longer in danger of applying the local colour on the surface of his music. There are moments of obvious parody, when he lays on the harmonies with deliberate recklessness, but elsewhere he manages to draw every detail of atmosphere and characterization from the hints that lie waiting within the few short bars of the folk-tunes. And he misses none of the opportunities Shakespeare has given him: Falstaff's demand for a cup of sack is enlivened by its violent change of key when he finds they have put lime in it, and there is an ominous darkness as he mutters 'a bad world, I say'; with a touch, Holst conveys the twinge of old age that seizes him in the middle of his drink. The slow deliberation of 'I call thee coward! I'll see thee damned!' gains added weight from its morris 'capers', and there are dramatic possibilities in the modulations of 'Give me them that will face me': the abrupt enharmonic change which deflates the balloon of Falstaff's boasting is like a subtle parody of Holst's 'Early Horrors' of the eighteen-nineties. Repeated staccato quavers on cellos and double-basses, bouncing between mediant and dominant, convey the absurdity of Falstaff's 'I am eight times thrust through the doublet'. Later on in the tune, these quavers acquire passing notes that turn them into legato semiquavers, and when Falstaff finds it increasingly difficult to make his swaggering lies sound convincing, the semiquavers are played in three keys at once, lending a hint of desperation to his statement that 'they were bound, every man of them; or I am a Jew else, an Ebrew Jew'. He recovers his balance in time for the unflustered recollection of 'I have pepper'd two of them'. There is a nimble touch of characterization here: the six-eight rhythm causes him to hold up the arrival of the second half of the word 'pepper'd', and the soft plop of the explosive 'p' is pricked out with a pizzicato discord.

The smooth alternation of dominant and supertonic suits the calm tone of voice of the Prince's 'Breathe awhile, and then to it again', and it is welcome as a tranquillo counter-subject to the enormity of Falstaff's lying assertion, 'By the Lord, I knew ye as well as he that made ye', a sentence that sounds as if it might have been specially written to fit the opening bars of 'Trunkles'. This tune becomes more and more appropriate when it expands into majestic 'capers' at 'I for a valiant lion', breaking off into its quick 'galley' step for the muttered aside 'but by the Lord, lads, I am glad you have the money'. This is the neatest moment in the whole opera, but its full flavour can only be enjoyed by those who know the ins and outs of a morris dance.

When Mistress Quickly announces that there is a messenger from the Court, a sudden change in the orchestral colour reminds us that it is getting late. Falstaff asks—'What doth gravity out of his bed at midnight?' and there is an undisguised weariness in the quotation from 'Old Noll's Jig', as violas and bassoons lean over with a gesture that has the ache and the satisfaction of a yawn behind it. The spacing of the chord at the word 'midnight' has an extraordinary effect on the brief silence that follows: we are conscious that the whole of Eastcheap has been asleep for some time, and that it is only in the tavern that there has been such a noise going on. For a while there is quietness: Falstaff is able to look back reminiscently on the days before he grew old and fat. 'I could have crept into any alderman's thumb-ring' he mutters, and the pizzicato double-bass under the held pianissimo of the flute and bassoons matches the imagination of the moment.

It was a mistake to use 'Old Noll's Jig' as an accompaniment for the parlante discussion about Percy and Glendower: the tune is too eventful for background music, and we are tempted to listen with both ears until we realize that Falstaff is talking about someone who 'runs o' horseback up a hill perpendicular', and then we wish we had given our whole attention to the words. It is an example of one of the fundamental failings of the opera: there are far too many excitements happening all the time. The writing is more economical in the ridiculous dialogue between the Prince and Falstaff when they rehearse Hal's interview with his father; here the tunes help the words instead of hindering them. As Falstaff, with a three-two maestoso gesture, commands the nobility to stand aside, Mistress Quickly breaks into her cackle of 'O Jesu, this is excellent sport, i' faith!' to an animato two-four: wood-wind and muted trumpets tongue their staccato semiquavers in the simultaneous keys of A and F, producing a startlingly lifelike impression of the hard edge of a laughter that is vulgar, warm-hearted, and weary. It is the bright, forced gaiety of one who enjoys a good joke with a customer but who wishes, all the same, that it were closing time.

Holst's worst error of judgement was in choosing legato six-eight tunes with long, flowing phrases for the stilted parody of 'I do not speak to thee in drink but in tears, not in pleasure but in passion', and for the burlesque rhetoric of 'Wherein [is he] cunning, but in craft? Wherein crafty but in villany?' The words lose their point, being dragged away from their intended course, and the tunes suffer when their sweeping lines are yoked in such unsuitable partnership.

This obvious weakness is shown up by his neat use of recurring staccato fragments in the more jaunty dances: the exuberant downward leap of a diminished octave might have been purposely invented for the old fat man 'with a pudding in his belly'. And there is a subtle suggestion of a hiccup in the tune that announces Doll Tearsheet's arrival: before she has had time to open the door we are certain she will be looking somewhat the worse for wear when she comes in.

The tune of 'Heartsease', on muted strings, is appropriate for Doll's tipsily amorous: 'Come, I'll be friends with thee, Jack.' When Falstaff rises, the hiccup becomes elongated into his legato 'Kiss me, Doll', the violins following his rubato and stretching their two octaves over his head, before subsiding on to their dominant ninth.

When the Prince enters disguised as a drawer, he sings a contemplative setting of 'Devouring Time, blunt thou the lion's paws', while Falstaff shows his disapproval of the words by interrupting them with a fortissimo rendering of 'When Arthur first'. Its rollicking twelve-eight is not able to prevent the Prince from singing a second 'verse' of his song, to the words 'When I do count the clock that tells the time'. The two tunes follow their independent course, Doll Tearsheet taking turns with Falstaff in his seemingly interminable ballad. There is a short break when muted trumpets play a distant soldiers' march, and then the songs continue as a quintet. But here Holst made the mistake of using his characters as so many 'voices' in an ensemble: he wanted to have the sonnet in three-part counterpoint in close imitation, and so he made Mistress Quickly join the Prince's tenor and Poins's bass, quite forgetting that Shakespeare would never have allowed his lively hostess to sing such lines as 'Do whate'er thou wilt, swift-footed Time, To the wide world and all her fading sweets'. The music becomes more and more complicated as the distant march is heard through the intricacies of the counterpoint, and Falstaff gets so excited over his story of Sir Lancelot that he bursts into canon in augmentation at 'Forthwith he struck his neck in two'. It is devastatingly clever, but there is no dramatic justification for such a network of difficulties. Holst must have realized this, for he has pencilled in an optional cut in the manuscript full score.

The arrival of ancient Pistol to the solo tuba's morris 'galley' was a happy thought. So was Mistress Quickly's quotation from Falstaff's earlier boasting in three keys, when she declares that she'll have no swaggerers in the Boar's Head. The excitement increases with the hostess's rising indignation, the wood-wind chattering together in a staccato three-part canon. Although their tonguing is as light as a succession of pin-pricks it is difficult to listen to the singers' words, for the ear is completely captivated by the counterpoint. But alas, it is just at this moment that Falstaff chooses to say, 'You may stroke him as gently as a puppy greyhound: he'll not swagger with a Barbary hen, if her feathers turn back in any show of resistance'. Once more Holst has crowded too many riches into the space of a few seconds.

Pistol's entry is memorable for the ritualistic solemnity of his molto maestoso greeting. Its solemnity is too much for Doll Tearsheet, and the rapid quavers of her tantrums betray her overwrought state of mind. These quavers are tossed to and fro and hurled upside down and sprinkled with bitonal clashes that lend additional spice to such exclamations as 'you basket-hilt stale juggler, you'. There is a simultaneous outburst as Pistol protests, 'I'll see her damned', and Doll scornfully retaliates, 'He lives upon mouldy stewed prunes and dried cakes'. It is no wonder that Mistress Quickly has to shriek out 'for God's sake be quiet'. In the unnatural calm that follows there is time to notice that Pistol is *very* drunk: he becomes maudlin as he sings of the seven stars, *con espress.*, to a wickedly luscious neo-modal string passage. The quarrel is renewed: swords are drawn, and some of the words are inevitably lost in the bustle of bitonality. When Pistol is at last thrown out of the house the music returns to a pleasantly befuddled six-eight, while the two women take it in turns to wipe the sweat off Falstaff's face. But they are interrupted by the muted trumpets of the soldiers' march: Bardolph says that everyone is asking for Sir John Falstaff. 'Now comes in the sweetest morsel of the night, and we must hence and leave it unpicked', sighs Falstaff, to a *senza misura* variant of 'Heartsease'. One can imagine the glee with which Holst put in those descending whole-tone dominant ninths.

The work ends, as all his comic operas end, with a rapid and intentional anticlimax.

Once again, his first-night audience was left in a state of bewilderment, unable to recover from the effects of so many excitements at once. The libretto alone, without any music, is too highly concentrated. Holst has managed to connect the different conversations so that the joins sound convincing, apart from one unfortunate slip that entails two sunsets on the same evening. But the Falstaff scenes were never intended to be picked out like plums and packed close together. And in the music there is very little relief from the brilliant onslaught of the counterpoint: the listening brain is stimulated to such feverish activity that at times one longs to echo Prince Hal's 'Breathe awhile, and then to it again'.

The work has seldom been revived. But it is impossible to believe that it will be allowed to be forgotten, for the vitality in the music is as fresh and sparkling as when it was written.

CHAPTER XII

THE TERZETTO AND THE BRIDGES PART-SONGS

(1924–6)

THE only chamber music he wrote, apart from his early student efforts, was the 1924 *Terzetto* for flute, oboe, and viola. This was the work that he found he had to listen to several times before he could make up his mind whether he liked it or not. In the end, he decided that he did.

The three conflicting keys may look uncongenial on paper, but the counterpoint draws them into an unforced relationship:

Ex. 56.

From these thin threads of thematic possibilities he constructs the whole of his first movement, ingeniously avoiding the strain of conflict so that the viola is able to play with a full tone and a warm conviction in its key of C while the other two climb unconcernedly down their ladders of D♭ and D, without harbouring any feeling of animosity towards each other. Later, when the three instruments draw together and move in crotchets, the chords they make, if played on the piano, sound like alternating first inversions of A♭ and F♯, followed by the second inversion of C. But these are not disconnected block harmonies indulging in 'false relations': they are three diatonic tunes, each voice keeping its own individuality. There is a perceptible difference in the flavour of the oboe's A♭ and the G♯ of the flute. It is startling enough to enable the ear to follow the three distinct lines of counterpoint, especially in the similar passage several bars later, where it is easier to disentangle the sounds owing to the clearly contrasted tone-colour at this particular level of pitch. But the startling flavour is never sufficiently acid to set the teeth on edge, or to destroy the balance of the underlying harmonic structure. At the end of the movement the three keys blend into one with complete unanimity: all tension dissolves in a lyrical outpouring that comes to rest with the oboe's lingering recollection of its first three notes of Ex. 56. Heard within the frame of the A and E¹ from the viola and flute, the final drift upwards from C¹ to D♭¹ brings with it the intense sadness of a cadence that is often heard in his last works.

The second of the two movements is a typical Holstian scherzo, with its prickly fourths hopping over the bar-line and gaining speed as they near the end of the sentence:

Ex. 57.

Un poco vivace

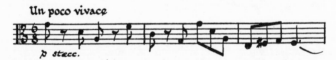

The unrelated keys bring a suggestion of whole-tone melancholy to the music, but it is a dry-eyed, steely edged melancholy, with none of the vague nostalgia of a whole-tone slither about it. The mood becomes even more resigned at the meno mosso, where the oboe has a cantabile two-four tune in A♭ while the flute ripples its way through a six-eight dance in E: the viola's pizzicato E♭ moves from one octave to another with leisurely persistence, knitting the two rhythms together and anchoring the two keys lest they should wander off and get lost on their separate journeys. He afterwards used the whole of this middle section in his *Double Concerto* for two violins and orchestra. As the fugue draws to an end, the rising scales that were first heard as quavers are hurried into semiquavers, their mixed tonality lending a mercurial quality to the music. Broken triads in contrary motion, which began by worrying each other in their uncomfortable proximity, no longer quote from Doll Tearsheet's quarrel with Pistol: their legato murmuring fills the air with the enchantment that he first discovered in the scherzo of the *Choral Symphony*.

The *Terzetto* gives a tantalizing hint of what he might have achieved if he had decided to write more chamber music. The lessons he learnt from this one short experiment helped him in his *Seven Part-Songs* for female voices and strings, with words by Robert Bridges. In the first song, *Say who is this with silver'd hair?*, he has matched the perplexity of the poem in the fragile melancholy of the voices' triads over the unwavering held note of the viola, and in the uncertainty of the hesitating quavers that totter from one side to the other. 'I did the first of the Bridges poems the moment I caught sight of the words', he wrote in 1925. 'Since when I've been wondering what they mean.' He never could decide what they were about. But he managed to draw out their magic, at the contrast between the pleasure of the young and the wisdom of the old, and at the 'deep divining' vision of the cellos' and basses' first entry, as they emerge from their long silence with the low murmuring voice of that mysterious being 'who knoweth things untold'. Not since the dialogue between Savitri and Death had he managed to convey an apprehensive dread with such naked counterpoint as at 'Whence came he hither all alone?' The voices and pizzicato violins flutter in anxious quavers at their uncomfortable canon in diminution, remote from the level of the arco augmentation, yet unable to escape from its all-pervading influence.

He found the right ingredients waiting for him in the words of *O Love, I complain*. An ordinary love song, *con espress.*, might have defeated him, but this 'complaint' just suited his needs, with its blend of irony and tenderness.

> Thou makest me fear
> The mind that createth,
> That loves not nor hateth
> In justice austere;
> Who, ere he make one,
> With millions toyeth,
> And lightly destroyeth
> Whate're is begun.

The leggiero 'lightly destroyeth' has an unheeding carelessness in the lingering labial of the voices and in the prick of the pizzicato strings, yet there is an underlying despair in the F major triad over the cello's held E. His frequent changes of time signature may look fussy on paper, but there is nothing fussy in the rhythm that follows the spoken shape and the unspoken image of the words:

Ex. 58.

The insolence of that last bar but one is unmistakable: it is a glimpse of a Holst who does not often allow himself to appear. There is a suggestion of the same insolence in *When first we met*, where the tune hovers for an instant over the faintly ironical drop of a diminished fifth at the 'irretrievable disaster' of love.

These Bridges songs have a welcome spontaneity about them, and they sound as if he was no longer quite so much afraid of sensuous beauty. In *Love on my heart from heaven fell*, a lyrical warmth flows through every note of the music, and in *Angel spirits of sleep* he melts into loveliness without losing his musical identity. But *Love on my heart* was only a temporary refuge: he had to struggle for several more years before he could be sure of reaching this spontaneous freedom whenever he needed it. And in *Angel spirits of sleep* the beauty has to rely on the unreality of a dream.

The last of the seven songs, *Assemble all ye maidens*, is an 'Elegy on a Lady whom grief for the death of her betrothed killed'. The sense of calamity can be heard in the bare Phrygian utterance of the opening solo, where the minor second and the tritone suggest the dismal cold and darkness of the 'late eventide'. When the *senza misura* moves between the framework of a fifth, the voice borrows its sad cadence from the end of the first movement of the *Terzetto*. At 'Sound flute and tabor', the music enters the landscape of the Grecian Urn. There is a memorable beauty in the strings' rising scale as it collects the voices one after another and carries them to the haven of their word 'Rest': it is the moment he had tried to reach in the *Ode to Death* at the height of 'Over the tree-tops I float thee a song'. As the funeral procession widens out into six-four, the austere fourths dissolve into Neptune-like harmonies:

Ex. 59.

There is an extraordinary effect of shifting tonality when the singers raise their torches and the changing level of light is reflected in the changing level of sound. By raising the C♯ in the ground bass to a D♮ he compels the listening ear to transform the held G♯ and D♯¹ to an A♭ and E♭¹. There is the same unearthly interchange at the end of the Elegy, when the chorus sings 'Rejoice for thou art near to thy possession': here the music reaches beyond the spoken thought, disclosing the piercing significance of that intangible possession.

This enharmonic change, which had already been hovering in his mind as long ago as in *Savitri*, was one of the sounds that helped to lead him to renewed warmth at the very end of his life.

CHAPTER XIII

FESTIVAL MUSIC FOR AMATEURS

(1925–8)

WHILE he was working at the *Seven Part-Songs* the outlines of a second Choral Symphony were already in his mind. He took the words from poems by George Meredith and he had got as far as planning the sequence of his four movements before he gave up all attempts to go on with the work. He has left several short fragments of the symphony in his note-books, and two or three pages of unfinished sketches, mostly from 'The Woods of Westermaine'. There is nothing on paper to suggest any indication of the last movement, where the words of 'Winter Heavens' might have drawn an answering recognition from the wintriness of his own chosen solitude.

He gave no reason for abandoning the symphony. It was probably because he was feeling weary and depressed. Although he had recovered from the effects of his nervous breakdown, he was still finding it an effort to concentrate on composing every Sunday after a crowded week of teaching. And he was still tormented by the thought that his ideas were running dry. A symphony would have compelled him to face the unsolved problems of writing in extended form. Even with the help of the words, the task would probably have been too great a burden for him to bear at that time. He turned, instead, to the solace of writing for his pupils.

His short piano pieces owe most of their vitality to the Northumbrian folk-tunes on which they are founded. He has described how his *Toccata* has 'sincerely flattered' the old man with a worn-out hurdy-gurdy who used to play 'Newburn Lads' in Cheltenham in 1879. But the music goes deeper than the surface of his memory: the thin cracked notes of the pianissimo broken triads are like a jangling and tinny comment on the shimmering magic of 'Open wide the mind's cage door'.

He was happy enough with his peppery sprinkling of quaver fifths in *Chrissemas Day* and with his staccato fourths pecking their obstinate way off the beat in *The Shoemakker*, but he missed the cheerful abandon of these traditional tunes when it came to writing his choral ballet, *The Golden Goose*. It was founded on Grimm's fairy tale of the Princess who had never been able to laugh, and it was

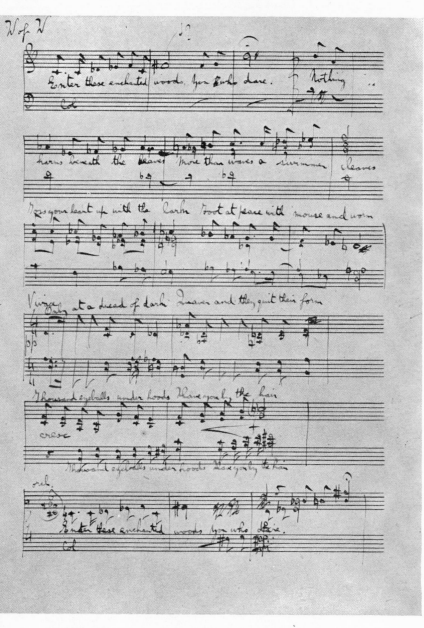

FRAGMENT OF A SECOND CHORAL SYMPHONY

written so that it could be performed out of doors at a Whitsun festival, with groups of characters improvising their movements. The music sounds like the work of a tired brain. The familiar mannerisms are still there: the heralds' trumpet tune on rising fourths is used at twice the speed as a bustling background for the entry of the populace; its rows of first inversions over an ostinato tonic and dominant sound a bit too easy, as if they were habitually lying about and waiting to be picked up by two hands on a keyboard. The sweeping lines of the royal procession are good to sing, but the Mummers are given a tune which children had to learn laboriously, as they found it difficult to deal with all those fourths and seconds. It is also difficult for them to steer through the rallentando at the end of each verse: keeping together while gradually slowing down during four naked bars of unison six-eight is a problem at the best of times, but it becomes much worse when the singers are supposed to be acting: they have to dig themselves in on each beat of the bar, with the result that the phrasing becomes laboured. It is a rare instance of unpractical writing. There is an effective moment of contrast where the Princess and her ladies mope and look miserable while 'vainly awaiting some beguiling', their consecutive triads drifting round A major and yawning against the sustained F$\natural$ of the English horn and cellos. The Human Organ can also be very effective, for the Showman—a thinly disguised Wizard—'plays' the organ with frenzied movements of his feet and hands, while two of his gnomes 'blow' the odd-looking instrument, using a singer's arm as a handle; meanwhile sopranos, altos, and basses, dressed up as organ pipes, stand fixed and immovable, practising monotonous technical exercises to the vowel sounds 'ah', 'ee', and 'ho'.

When three girls catch sight of the magical Golden Goose, there is an angular fragment of a tune which sounds as if it might have strayed from one of his neo-classical experiments:

Ex.60.

The uncomfortable change of stress is difficult to move to, and the awkward intervals refuse to sing themselves in the inner ear: the dancer has to count out each quaver's worth instead of letting go and allowing the steps to phrase themselves. This sort of writing is somewhat forbidding on a bank-holiday afternoon, and it is a relief to be allowed to get back to the singable procession and to be assured that everyone is going to live happily ever afterwards.

A second choral ballet, *The Morning of the Year*, was written for the English Folk-Dance Society. It was meant to be 'a representation of the mating ordained by Nature to happen in the spring of each year'. The work was built on a foundation of morris and country-dance movements, and it was inevitable that some of the music should sound like imitation folk-tunes. But there was no need for it to sound so dull. Occasionally there is a short passage where the imagination is clearly recognizable:

Ex.61.

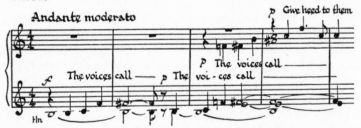

Such moments are rare. The Voice of Nature, represented by a chorus divided into groups on either side of the stage, should have drawn magic from every line, but the singers' modal phrases are ironed out flat by their non-committal crotchets. The pseudo-morris tunes are sadly lacking in shape and purpose, and the long crescendo of the Mating Dance, relying on its indispensible fourths, finds very little to feed on. The work sounds as if it might have been written by one of his imitators.

It was not that he was bored with writing for amateurs: he had worked at these two choral ballets with genuine enthusiasm, and he had put every available ounce of energy into them both. But he was unable to shake off the accumulated weariness of years and years of overwork. Without realizing it, he was getting entangled in administrative details, and there was no relaxation to be found in the deliberate kindliness and good-humour with which he filled his teaching days. He could only escape from the worry and the strain when he withdrew still farther into that other remote region of ceaselessly exploring thought—a region that seemed to be getting lonelier as each year went by. He had already begun grappling in his mind with the vast emptiness of *Egdon Heath*, and he was finding it more and more difficult to reconcile his two lives. It would have been a mistake to cut out the teaching life altogether, for he still needed his amateurs' help, almost as much as they needed his. But the simple works he wrote for them during these tired years only come alive when the words breathe the same air as *Egdon Heath*.

Among the short anthems and motets belonging to this time, it is only in *The Evening Watch* that he reaches a mystical fervour. This setting of Vaughan's Dialogue between the Body and Soul is built up almost entirely of superimposed fourths, but they are not the unthinking consecutive fourths that had become such a habit. Here they are a source of strength, drawing their balanced symmetry from the severe outlines of the poem. The Soul's first words, 'Go, sleep in peace', give an impression of a tranquillity that is both flowing and static, and Holst's warning, 'no variation from sempre *pp*', ensures that there will be no warmth or excitement in these rising phrases as the eight voices spread outwards from their unison. The calm of the music is broken into by the Body's anxious questioning; there is compassionate impatience in the Soul's exclamation, 'Ah go', as it echoes that same struggle which could be heard in the second of the *Four Songs* for voice and violin.

This intensity is lacking in the other short choral works. In Bridges' *Eternal Father* the feathery leggiero of the trebles' and altos' repeated Alleluias lifts the anthem into lyrical grace, but the maestoso tune in *Man born to toil* suggests that he had been doing this sort of thing far too long, and in *Sing me the men* it is disconcerting to hear the well-worn consecutive sevenths between the tune and the bass, with layers of consecutive fourths sandwiched between them: this was a device that could be turned on much too easily in moments of exhaustion. The same mild and mannered harmonies are allowed to fill whole pages of the incidental music for *The Coming of Christ*, which he wrote for a Whitsun festival in Canterbury Cathedral. Owing to the acoustics in the nave, the writing had to be as straightforward as possible, which meant he was unable to rely on the help that counterpoint might have brought him. Much of the music is uneventful; the voices declaim effortlessly, following the shape of the verses and floating over a mellow pool of pleasant-sounding flattened sevenths and consecutive fifths and held pedal notes. Perhaps he realized that he was repeating himself, for *The Coming of Christ* is the last work he wrote in this all-too-familiar idiom.

Although the *Moorside Suite* for brass band seems to be looking back reminiscently to the folk-song settings of twenty years ago, the music has vitality, and it looks forward as well as back. There is a rare tenderness in the opening of the Nocturne:

Ex. 62.

These falling sixths, recalling the poignancy of *I love my love*, are instinctively turning towards the *Lyric Movement* of five years later. The last movement of the suite is like a mature comment on the early *Marching Song* of 1908: it is a fitting acknowledgement of a twenty years' debt of gratitude for the solid and companionable help that folk-songs had brought him. They had been a refuge on so many occasions. But in 1928 he could afford to do without their help, for he had already found his own secure refuge in the empty solitude of *Egdon Heath*.

CHAPTER XIV

EGDON HEATH

(1927)

THE mood of *Egdon Heath* had grown out of a sentence in Hardy's novel, 'The Return of the Native', where the heath is described as 'a place perfectly accordant with man's nature—neither ghastly, hateful, nor ugly; neither commonplace, unmeaning, nor tame; but, like man, slighted and enduring; and withal singularly colossal and mysterious in its swarthy monotony'.

This was Holst's idea of beauty. Its uncompromising denial of ease and charm was perfectly in accordance with his own nature: he was by rights a native of that sparsely populated country of the mind.

In his search for this rare beauty he had been driven farther and farther into solitude, but there is no hint of exile in the loneliness of *Egdon Heath*: it is a home-coming.

Men [wrote Hardy] have oftener suffered from the mockery of a place too smiling for their reason than from the oppression of surroundings over-sadly tinged. Haggard Egdon appealed to a subtler and scarcer instinct, to a more recently learnt emotion, than that which responds to the sort of beauty called charming and fair.

Indeed, it is a question if the exclusive reign of this orthodox beauty is not approaching its last quarter. The new Vale of Tempe may be a gaunt waste in Thule: human souls may find themselves in closer and closer harmony with external things wearing a sombreness distasteful to our race when it was young. The time seems near, if it has not actually arrived, when the chastened sublimity of a moor, a sea, or a mountain will be all of nature that is absolutely in keeping with the moods of the more thinking among mankind.

The opening theme for muted double-basses is so quiet and unde-monstrative that it scarcely interrupts the surrounding silence:

Ex. 63.

Although the even crotchets are written in seven-four, the first thirteen notes belong to a single phrase that knows no pulse or division. Nor is there any stress in the relation of the pitch of one note and the next: the tune moves on its unhindered way, legato and senza portamento, passing through G minor and B♭ minor but without being claimed by either key. The phrase, however, is not in the least shapeless or meandering: there is a clear relationship between one note and the next, but it is a remote relationship. When the flutes and bassoons move towards each other they bring the calm assurance of the opening of *Venus*; but this is a colder vision and 'a more recently learnt emotion'. The divisi strings creep in one after another, echoing the basses' rising crotchets in canon, and leading to the poco animato. Here the six-note phrase, founded on the third bar of Ex. 63, floats across the seven-four bar-lines, alternating between muted and unmuted violins, while the last lingering notes of the basses' falling phrase are taken over by flute and bassoon and horn. Each legato line is so complete in itself that it can never be broken up and compelled to fit into the beats of a bar: there can be no counting the clock that tells this time as it passes away without effort and without desire or regret.

At the return to Tempo I the muted strings stretch across four octaves for the opening theme, while the unmuted strings hold an E♭ pedal, giving an overwhelming sense of space to the tune which began as a solitary wandering. When the strings play the first half of the tune in canon, their counterpoint calls forth harmonies belonging to 'surroundings over-sadly tinged':

Ex. 64.

At [2] we hear the first notes of the inevitable 'sad procession': the music has left the remote distances of time and space and has turned to consider man, 'slighted and enduring'. There is a sudden restlessness in the second violins' continuous quaver figure at the Poco Allegro: it is in a true fifteen-eight, not a series of triplets in five-four, and there is an urgency about it and a hint of despair that is increased by the entry of the first violins an augmented fourth higher:

Ex. 65.

It is extraordinarily like the sound of the wind in the grass on a high, open moor. But *Egdon Heath* is not an impressionistic tone-poem: each note of the music grows out of the colossal and mysterious mood that inspired it, and if these fifteen-eight quavers sound like the wind on the moor, they also sound like the buffetings of conflicting currents of thought in a mind that is mercilessly exposed to every storm. The underlying harmonic structure of the passage is that same clash of F♯ major and C major which brought the warning of suffering in the Prelude of *The Hymn of Jesus* (Ex. 36). Here, instead of the tension being superimposed in block harmony, it has been created out of a single line of melody.

At three bars before ③ the oboe has a tune which focuses the restless urgency of the violins' fifteen-eight and leads to the rising

Heard in this context, these four notes contain the essential agony of the pursuing trumpets in *Mars*.

At ④ the whole orchestra remembers the sad procession and moves forward passionately on to a held discord through which the trumpet quotes from the opening theme in a piercing fortissimo. The climax is reached on a first inversion of E♭ major, a chord which on other occasions can sound so very mild: here it loses all trace of former associations and becomes terrifying. As the strings draw out their protest on the first three notes of the opening theme, there is a lessening of the tension: the wood-wind moves to and fro on an echo of the piercing discord: the passion of the held strings dissolves until the violins are left on a high pianissimo question-mark which is answered by the sad procession of the trombones and trumpets.

The dolce at five bars after ⑥ is the nearest approach to lyrical beauty in the whole of *Egdon Heath*: its flowing quavers try to escape, but the elegiac mood of the procession persists, until a vehement descending scale breaks off and leaves the oboe chanting in untroubled serenity. All movement ceases: a held triad on flutes and English horn is all that remains of that approaching clamour, while the oboe lifts its phrase into a region that knows the contemplative calm of a 'Pange lingua'.

There is a pause at the end of this brief chant on a quietly held fourth on D and G—a desolate sound that haunts the music for the next thirty-four bars. It forms the thin, insubstantial framework of the Adagio, where the low-lying flutes play a lament in fourths, dwelling on their A♭ D♭¹, through the sustained D G¹ of the *ppp* second violins. The 'chastened sublimity' of the music sounds even more remote nine bars later, where violas and cellos play the lament at the same level of pitch, with a strained intensity in their pianissimo, while the basses hold the D♮ on a high harmonic and the first violins move from G¹ to F¹ and back again, their wraith of sound recalling the trumpet's piercing outcry after 4. At the andante six-eight the flutes and bassoons transform the lament into a melancholy dance. It is an unforgettable sound: it holds the essence of the magic ritual of the morris, a ritual that tries in its own way to withstand the slighting forces of nature. This was the mood he had been searching for in *The Morning of the Year*. Here he finds it.

The dance leads straight into the return of the opening theme, spread across all the octaves of the muted strings, over a pedal G. This unobtrusive return is an example of Holst's economical way of getting where he wanted at a moment's notice, without any signs of wear or tear. Many listeners find it upsetting to be carried up into his swiftly moving thought with so little preparation. But there is nothing abrupt about this return: the warning was given twenty bars ago, when the violins moved to and fro between G¹ and F¹ with haunting persistence.

At the end, the conflicting elements in the music are brought together and reconciled: with the final rising fourths in lento minims the agonized trumpet-call becomes transformed into a tranquil gesture that draws aside the curtains of time and space before waiting, unafraid, at the farthest solitary edge of existence. It is Holst's answer to the nightmare of that questioning pursuit. The tranquil gesture was heard long ago, in the *Hymn to the Dawn* and in the *Ode on a Grecian Urn*, but there the curtains were drawn on a sunlit landscape at the beginning of a busy day. In *Egdon Heath* there is no sunshine. The landscape is empty, and there is no one left to make a new beginning of the questioning.

There is nothing 'inhuman' in this emptiness. It is not a denial, but a summing-up, for the music could never have happened without all those other experiences: the brass band's march; the 'insolent slave' of *O Love, I complain*; Mistress Quickly's hard-edged laughter; Fancy 'opening wide the mind's cage door'; the Perfect Fool yawning in the face of beauty; the fierce exaltation of 'Divine Grace is dancing'; the weary greyness of 'Age after age her tragic empires rise'; the clamour of *Mars*; Savitri's triumph over Death; and 'good old Wagnerian' *Sita*, who had learnt that the gods were powerless without the help of slighted and enduring man.

CHAPTER XV

THE TWELVE SONGS AND THE DOUBLE CONCERTO

(1929)

Egdon Heath gave him new strength and filled him with a sense of exhilaration. He knew it was the best thing he had written. But the exhilaration only lasted a very short time. His strength was worn down by the perpetual strain of overwork, and the year which followed was a year full of weariness. Teaching took all his energy, as well as nearly all his time, and he had to use the hours when he should have been resting in forcing himself to go on composing. At last he realized that he was defeated, and he decided to give up the struggle for a while. He spent several months in Italy, wandering about in the sunshine, away from all thoughts of teaching and organizing, and by the time he got back to England he was longing to begin composing again.

The *Twelve Songs*, with words by Humbert Wolfe, were a new adventure: more than twenty years had gone by since he had last tried to write a song for solo voice and piano. It was also a new adventure to be setting poems that were less severe than usual. Opening the songs at random, on the first page of *Rhyme* it is startling to find such unaccustomed images as 'beauty's fairy granges' and 'her lost elfin-bells': surely this can have nothing to offer the discriminating Holst? But the last verse is more reassuring:

> Rhyme
> by your clear chime
> we climb
> clean out of space and time,
> and the small earth behind us
> can neither lose or find us,
> set free
> in your eternity.

It is his own country, after all, though it is a different language and a different approach.

There is an unashamed lyricism in *Rhyme*, and there is also a sensuous delight in being pianistic, which is a thing that had never happened since the far-off days of his first apprenticeship: the ripples of chromatically descending semiquavers would have been avoided at any other time during the last twenty years, so long and arduous had been his struggle to escape from these very sounds.

In *A Little Music* he dips into the once-rejected mood of the 'nightingale' verse in the Finale of the *Choral Symphony*, where the rose-scented daisies had made him feel so uncomfortable that he had had to alter several harmonies that were too mild and luscious for his taste. But here he remains unperturbed by the lusciousness of the long-drawn-out dominant ninth through which the 'fishes of emerald dive for the moon'. *The Floral Bandit* is equally luscious, and he indulges whole-heartedly in a pianistic orgy of broken dominant sevenths for the accompaniment of the blackbird's song, without betraying any symptoms of a guilty conscience. He also indulges in borrowing fragments from other men's music, and manages to prevent the quotations from sticking out of the framework of the song. At 'the small language of the rain', there is a recollection of 'Jardins sous la pluie' in the persistent pattering of the semiquavers, yet those descending crotchets that drip downwards through the shower are unmistakably Holstian. The quotation from 'Who is Sylvia' merges just as easily into the form and texture of the song: even the two-part invention for the 'old thin clavichord' fits into the picture, for all its eighteenth-century formality. The song is not important in itself, but in 1929 it mattered a great deal to Holst's state of mind that he should have been able to plunge with abandon into such fantastic unexpectedness.

The ripples of sound in *The Dream City* are nearer to his usual economy of expression: a falling D to C washes against a rising E♭ to A♭ and instantly suggests the two cross-currents of thought in the lapping of the river and the lapping of the dream. When these ripples emerge on to the cool impact of the word 'night', the moment of enchanted suspense holds in it the darkness and disguise of his remembered stretch of the Thames at Hammersmith. This is the language he had learnt in the Bridges *Part-Songs*: it can be heard again in *Persephone*, where the Phrygian tune is swept along on waves of alternating enharmonic changes, with an urgency in its recurring flattened supertonic. In several of the Humbert Wolfe songs he uses a technical device that he had thought of many years before, when he had been unable to make satisfactory use of it owing to his lack of harmonic security. He lets his legato phrases rise in one key, change at the crest of the slow wave, and sink in another key until they have found the level of pitch where they began. In his earlier attempts he had made the mistake of burdening each subtle inflection by adding modulating harmonies, but here, as in *Journey's End*, he cuts out all unnecessary accompaniment and sustains a chord that will share some of the needs of the beginning and end of the curve of the tune, without doing violence to the passing notes that lie between. He uses the same device in *Now in these Fairylands*, where the voice keeps within its octave and changes its course without effort, while the held chords collect the essential harmonies of each stage of the journey, helping to draw the singer from one step to the next. In *Things Lovelier*, these chords have shrunk to such bare skeletons that they might seem at first to be almost too gaunt and forbidding. But they convey all that he needs in the groping of the 'hands stretched like a blind man's hands' and in the controlled recognition of 'you cannot dream things lovelier'. There is the same economy in *The Thought*, where the thinly supported *senza misura* is in keeping with the brief statement of the poem. At the words 'I will hold you in a thought without moving spirit or desire or will', there is an illuminating contrast between 'spirit' with its clear, frostily chaste D♭ F C¹, and 'desire', with its stress and strain as it is pulled two ways by the chord of D♭ F A C♯¹ E¹, and 'will' with its deliberately built-up strength of D♮ G C♮¹. The frugality of the writing leaves many listeners cold and unmoved, since it provides no easy outlet for the emotions, but demands an imagination as penetrating as his own.

Not all the songs achieve this clarity: the declamation in *Envoi* is unconvincing, for the recitative is not dramatic enough in itself to carry the weight of a forte rising to a fortissimo. And there is a lack of intensity in the series of consecutive sevenths when 'evening slowly by hill and wood perfects her holy solitude'. These minor sevenths have an equally dampening effect on the resigned tranquillity of *In the street of lost time*, and it is difficult to avoid the unwelcome associations in the added sixth of the final chord: Holst was spared this particular distress, for he died before the cadence had become a blustering byword.

Of the twelve Humbert Wolfe songs, the poem which came nearest to his own way of thought was *Betelgeuse*. The brightest star in Orion was remote enough in time and space to call up an answering remoteness in his music. The voice, in unhurried crotchets, sings an aloof, contemplative chant; never settling for an instant, yet never unsettled; moving continuously, but without endeavouring to arrive. The falling A♭ hangs poised over the bare octaves of the ostinato, while they draw aside the curtains, as in *Egdon Heath*, with an immense indifference:

Ex. 66.

At 'Space is a wind that does not blow', a fourth on A♭ spreads through the ostinato, and tolls with slow persistence until the end of the song, recalling that insubstantial held D and G in *Egdon Heath*: it draws out the muted answering octaves until they stretch farther into the distance. The sudden three strokes of the marcato A♭ shatter the *ppp* with a warning that is as inescapable as the first notes of the clanging bells in *Saturn*: the air is still vibrating during the desolation of the *senza misura* assurance that 'nothing joys or grieves'. There is a terrifying naked intensity in 'nor ghost of evil or good haunts the gold multitude': for an instant the voice is left solitary on the E♭ of 'haunts' before the first inversion of D♭ clutches at it; then the sound dissolves with the grief of the singer's descending phrase in C♯ minor. The piano is the right instrument here: nothing else could suggest such an involuntary fading away into silence. The last few notes of the quiet ostinato share the unanxious gaze which follows that other tranquil rising fourth at the end of *Egdon Heath*.

It was just after he had been listening to the first public performance of the *Twelve Songs* that Holst was seized with a profound dissatisfaction which brought him very near to despair. He was so tired that he was scarcely able to hear a note of the songs: he felt imprisoned in a cold region where his brain was numb and his spirit was isolated. It happened that the programme ended with the Schubert Quintet in C and, hearing the warmth of the music, he began to thaw. And while thawing he began to realize all that he had lost by clinging to his austerity. He had reached far into the distance, but he had missed the warmth of the Schubert Quintet, and it seemed as if that warmth might after all be the only thing worth having.

This was not a sudden realization: it was the climax of years of unspoken doubt. He had obviously felt the need for ease and spontaneity while working at the Bridges *Part-Songs*. But it was not until he had written *Egdon Heath* that his dissatisfaction became so acute. In *Egdon Heath* his thought had journeyed to the farthest rim of solitude, and having reached understanding, he knew that the next step must be a return. Many years before this he had set out with the intention of trying to keep his mind as clear as the mind of a mathematician, never allowing his work to get entangled in 'the domestic emotions'. It had been the price he had had to pay for following his vision. And it had been worth it, for it had led him to *Egdon Heath*, which was as near to perfection as he could reach. But having got there, he discovered that it was not enough to have been an observer. It was not enough that his piercing imagination should have recognized the note of endurance in Mistress Quickly's high-pitched laughter. It was not enough that he should have guessed at the secret of those tottering, prying footsteps in *Say who is this?*, or that he should have penetrated behind the untroubled gaze of the Princess and the Perfect Fool. The time had now come when he had got to allow his music to become involved in the painful necessity of compassion. Perhaps he had realized this as long ago as in 1923, when he had discovered that Keats was his favourite poet and 'the only writer with the soul of an artist'—a remark which even his closest friends found too naïve to be tolerated. In 1929 he knew that there could be no escape and that he had got to let the warmth of the Schubert Quintet thaw him to the very bone. He never tried to put this feeling into words, but he must have been aware that there was more in his dissatisfaction than the weariness of overwork. And he must have known that he could not go on for very much longer writing music that was cold and dry and solitary. But it was difficult to know how to find warmth. Technically he was not nearly ready for it. The Humbert Wolfe songs had helped by breaking down the surface crust of his austerity, but they had not gone deep enough. His next work, the *Double Concerto* for two violins and orchestra, struggles to get nearer to the needed warmth, though at first glance the writing appears to be as dry and brittle as ever.

The concerto is fugal in construction and bitonal in language: the three movements, following without a break, are inseparably linked to each other. The Scherzo plunges abruptly into the ostinato: it is another example of a restless fragment adjusted to arrive on a different stress at each repetition, and it needs to be phrased with

unsparing sympathy to avoid the danger of letting it disintegrate into
a series of sniffs on the empty beats of the bar. The persistent
alternation between E and F helps to bind the tonality together by
scattering the self-assertion of any individual line of counterpoint:
the two notes are shared between the contending voices so that, as in
Ex. 67, E minor fluctuates without any fuss through what amounts
to B♭ major and C♯ major:

Ex. 67.

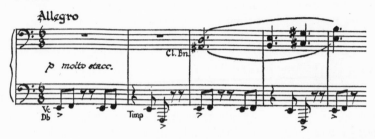

The excitement increases as the rising phrase on the wood-wind
is speeded up: sandwiched into the silences between the notes of the
ostinato, it prepares the way for the solo violin's entry of the fugal
subject:

Ex. 68.

This remoulding the shape of the descending phrase is the same
device that he uses in the Humbert Wolfe songs: here it delivers him
from the borrowed formality of the 1923 *Fugal Concerto*, while
allowing him to keep to the fundamental relationship of tonic and
dominant, without which his chippy, scampering subject would be
meaningless. The first half of the counter-subject is a good example
of his particular kind of ingenuity: it quotes the opening of Ex. 68
inverted, and by filling the subject's empty gaps it links the separate
fragments into six continuous quavers in a bar and conveys an
impression of leaping major sevenths and augmented fourths, although each voice is moving stepwise in its own path. The second half
of the counter-subject, with its sweeping rise and fall of three legato
crotchets in a bar, borrows some of the elasticity of *Mercury*, and
encourages the lower strings to play the subject in augmentation.

There is an episode that is a staccato version of the second half of the counter-subject in diminution: the two soloists casually toss their fragments from one to the other with Holst's usual conversational interchange between C and D♭, while clarinets and bassoon help to tie their fluttering remarks together by holding a second inversion of D♭ and then sinking smoothly down on to a second inversion of C— a sound that is also to be heard in *Hammersmith* and the 1934 *Scherzo*. The new six-eight tune bears an unmistakable resemblance to those gawky Wizards who flounder their way through *Uranus* and *The Perfect Fool*. This particular tune seems to date still farther back: its raucous whole-tone scale would have been thoroughly at home in the discarded *Phantastes* of 1911. The second soloist's legato four-four is also looking back to the days of his apprenticeship: the quasi-folk-song rises from a whole-tone phrase which is still shaking off the last of the *Phantastes* mood, and melts into pure Dorian, being answered in six-eight by the first soloist while flutes and bassoons steal in with their smooth and tender harmonies. But the espressivo is only allowed to last for a very few bars, before we are snatched back for a recapitulation of Ex. 67. These brief glimpses of lyrical beauty have a tantalizing effect on the listener and give the impression that Holst was shying away from his feelings. But he needed the sudden changes of mood. At the double bar he borrows a whole section from the second movement of the *Terzetto*; the music treads a soothing pattern without travelling anywhere in particular, but there is magic in it, and all too soon we are led away from the enchantment back to the scherzando fugue. The coda scurries from one tune to another— we are scarcely launched on the third entry of the subject before the *Phantastes* tune is heard on the first solo violin, no longer gawky and obnoxious, but acquiescent, and tranquilly blending into the surrounding leggiero. It gives way to the six-eight folk-song which finally dissolves into its four-four version, *con espress.* and poco adagio. It is in F♯ minor, and it floats its way up to an unexpected C♮^{11} over the held A and C♯^{1} of the orchestral strings: it falls back to E^1, but rises again to C♮^{11}, and this time it is no longer unexpected; it is a recognition of an awaited tenderness. As the pianissimo A C♯^{1} fades on to an A♭ D♭^{1}, the soloist's high C♮^{11} sinks for the last time to E^1 and the resolution becomes not only the summing up of all that has gone before, but also the gesture that leads into the Lament.

The form of this Scherzo is not easy to follow at a first hearing. We are only given a very short time to get into the new mood before we are abruptly lifted out of it. But this does not necessarily mean that the thought was disconnected in Holst's mind. To him, the sudden transitions were clear and inevitable. He was aware, however, of the difficulty of following his changes of mood: 'I begin to realise why people don't like my music', he once wrote from mid-Atlantic, when he had been memorizing his scores while walking up and down the deck for hours on end. He knew that he was often in danger of condensing his ideas until they could hardly be communicated. And he knew that his listeners were often bewildered, leaping the chasms between one thought and the next, without any hope of guessing at the hidden structure that was in his mind. But he remained unrepentant. Perhaps it is just as well he was unmoved by complaints or entreaties, for on the rare occasions when he tried to provide an easy step-ladder at the request of his friends, the result was always disastrous.

The apparent disjointedness of the first movement of the *Double Concerto* shows none of the signs of the compulsory snipping and stitching of a tired brain: there is a vitality in its restlessness that matches the urgency of his own discontent. But there is undoubtedly a lack of unity in the movement. He was more sure of himself in the Finale, where he could rely on the help of the Ground. The first movement, however, is a more courageous attempt to reach the next stage of the journey that was to lead him to the unfinished symphony of 1934. And the three movements have to be considered as a whole. The concerto is continuous, and it is the friction in the Scherzo that brings about the mood of the Lament. Most of this second movement is an unaccompanied duo for the two soloists. The legato five-four Andante is aware of the need of warmth, but it remains aloof and melancholy as its balanced phrases draw their way through the separate keys which blend into one. The chromatic counter-subject breathes the desolation of the Prelude to the *Choral Symphony*, though it is a clearer air than the atmosphere hanging over those dank stretches of marshland. At the poco animato the desolation changes for an instant to the impassioned mood which was heard in the fire and ice of the *Four Songs* for voice and violin, and in the impatient 'Ah, go!' of the Soul's dialogue with the Body. At the Andante the melancholy returns, the flowing ostinato of the second violin lending a resignation to its sadness: as the ostinato dissolves into a descending scale of E minor, it drags the first violin's G♯ minor tune into augmented fourths and fifths that are poignant in their despair. When the orchestra creeps in it has a strangely soothing effect, for the sound is spread over four octaves instead of being closely concentrated in

I

the duo. Not that the music loses its melancholy: the chromatic poco animato is still whispering in 'heavy peacefulness', and the end of the movement reflects the sadness of the Bridges *Elegy*, as the orchestral strings hold their E♭ A♭ E♭[1] while the horn moves plaintively from D to C and back again. The violas' echo of this phrase is scarcely allowed to die away before the first solo violin seizes the two notes and whisks them into the persistent figure of the Variations on a Ground:

Ex. 69.

With characteristic energy, the second soloist interrupts with a blusterous three-four version of the Ground, pesante and fortissimo, making the G string shudder under its violent treatment.

The complicated cross-rhythm is controlled with the highest degree of skill and ingenuity: the two soloists intersperse comments in pizzicato double stops or in quaver passages that are neatly let into the outline of the pattern; the orchestra joins in with fragments of the dialogue in augmentation, until at the climax the ostinato is hammered out fortissimo under the once plaintive E♭ A♭ E♭[1] of the Lament. The poco meno mosso that follows is over-deliberate in its assertions: one cannot help wishing he could have allowed his five-four and seven-four tunes to follow the natural rise and fall of a dance, in the same way that his songs follow the natural inflection of the English language. Too often, however, the instrumental patterns are calculated moves in his clever brain. In these Variations he is still a long way from the surrender that was eventually to bring him freedom. The tension and relaxation are seldom an instinctive give-and-take, and it is impossible to avoid the suspicion that he was approaching his dance rhythms as if they were so many intellectual problems to be solved.

But in spite of moments of exasperation the third movement of the concerto is exciting to listen to. There is a characteristic passage where the dark colour of the staccato wood-wind chords over the pizzicato crotchets of the cellos and basses expresses a mood he had known for thirty years or more. The Walt Whitman-like march has now become speeded up almost out of recognition, but it keeps some of its dramatic power while hinting at the storm at sea in *Swansea Town*. And there is another return to an earlier Holst in a leggiero passage which has an unexpected charm reminiscent of the *St. Paul's Suite*.

With consummate skill he gathers his contrasting tunes together: the chromatic change of harmony at the meno mosso leads to a plaintive quotation from the Lament, the timpani dropping in for a sympathetic but determined utterance of the Ground which grows more and more insistent as the two soloists play their *Terzetto* tunes from the first movement. In the battle of wits, it is the Ground that wins: as the rhythm gets nearer it envelops the whole orchestra, banishing the *Terzetto* variation and working up to a fury of excitement until it emerges with a final gesture that sweeps all the conflict into a sudden silence.

CHAPTER XVI

THE TALE OF THE WANDERING SCHOLAR

(1929–30)

SOON after he had finished the *Double Concerto* he began work on his last opera, *The Tale of the Wandering Scholar*. He may possibly have realized that a dramatic story would help him to unravel some of his problems while he was still groping his way out of his discontent. Perhaps he was also aware of the unanswered challenge of the Troubadour in *The Perfect Fool*, who had brought a sense of reality to the music in the middle of all the restlessness. Stripped of the protection of parody, Holst was still unable to write an espressivo aria with a simple accompaniment. He could only approach his lyricism through counterpoint, and he had not yet travelled far enough to reach the unpretentious *molto cantabile* from which he had begun his journey in the eighteen-nineties.

At the time when he was writing *The Planets* he had had to rely on the primitive insistence of repeated rhythms and alternating block harmonies in his struggles to express what he wanted to say. Then, as he became more sure of his technique, he was able to move towards the freedom of counterpoint. But during the last few years this contra-puntal freedom had had its own dangers. There was the perilous delight of sorting out clever patterns, the apparent order that skilful part-writing could bring out of chaos, and the deceptive vitality caused by the friction of recurring discords. Most dangerous of all was the ease with which counterpoint could be turned out in moments of extreme weariness when it was a relief to get anything down on paper.

It is unlikely that Holst gave a thought to these dangers. He was too much in the thick of the struggle to realize what was happening. And he never allowed any theories about composition to prevent him from getting on with the job of writing his next work.

He decided to embark on another one-act comic opera, instinctively keeping hold of the support and protection of parody. By now he had learnt to avoid the mistake of taking a tightly packed libretto and overloading it with elaborate fugues. He chose to build his new cham-ber-opera on an incident in Helen Waddell's book, *The Wandering Scholars*, and he asked Clifford Bax to write the libretto for him.

The curtain goes up on the scene of a kitchen in a farm-house in France on an April afternoon in the thirteenth century. Alison, a buxom soprano, is scrubbing the table to an angular tune which recurs at intervals throughout the opera:

Ex. 70.

Her husband Louis puts an end to the scrubbing by singing a conventional six-eight quasi-folk-song about the spring (they have not been married for very long). Alison sends him off to town to the market, and as soon as he has gone she prepares to welcome her fat friend, Father Philippe, who is coming to see her. While waiting for him she also sings of the spring, lightly poising her sentences over a ground bass of four descending notes, until Father Philippe interrupts her by putting his head round the door. In the first couple of bars we learn all about him:

Ex. 71.

The characterization is clear and unmistakable: before he has had time to come in, we are already convinced that his eyes will screw up into little black beads when he is angry or frightened, that his fingers will be short and clammy, that he will roll gently from side to side as he walks, and that there will be grease stains on his cassock. The stuffed figures of *The Perfect Fool* were a thing of the past: Holst had not been acquainted with Falstaff for nothing. Father Philippe lives up to his reputation: as soon as he learns that Alison's

'honest husband' is away from home, he approaches with a determined accelerando and casts an eye over the food to a light epicurean
staccato from the English horn and the bassoon. When he pompously
asks: 'Am I wrong my daughter To think that I espy A wanton
elf of mischief sparkling in that eye?' the burlesque fits into the
texture of the music and sounds unselfconscious. Holst had learnt
how to be comic without letting his opera degenerate into an uncomfortable recollection of charades on a wet bank holiday, and he could
now manage to assimilate parody in his own writing. When Alison
says, 'Calm my unruly longings, Calm them, or I shall weep', the
pompousness of Father Philippe's four-four reproof turns to an
espressivo that has the merest suspicion of a tongue in its cheek: the
chord of F B♮ E♭' G♭' B♭' for the word 'weep' has lost its usual elegiac
grief and is wholly concerned with the delicate irony of the moment.

As Father Philippe's excitement rises, he breaks out into a pesante
version of the ground of Alison's first song, his heavy-footed ‘enthusiasm giving a blasphemous tug to the ghost of an Alleluia that haunts
the descending phrase. They are interrupted by the arrival of Pierre,
the Wandering Scholar, and Father Philippe hastily draws his hood
over his head and begins reading his book of devotions, while the
strings slide easily into their modal harmonization of a fragment of
plainsong. Its soothing murmur runs smooth as oil, but Pierre is not
to be deceived by it: he has come to beg for something to eat, and he
tells them his life-history in a lilting six-eight, accompanied by four
descending notes that are a variant of the Alleluia ground. Soon
Father Philippe can stand it no longer: he reads aloud from his book,
brilliantly twisting Pierre's tune into a menacing plainsong, and the
two keep up an uneasy cross-current: 'So great a passion I had to be
a scholar', sings Pierre, dwelling hopefully on his high G while gazing
into Alison's young eyes: 'et cum perverso perveteris' declaims Father
Philippe, marking each syllable with malicious intent and glancing
sideways from under his hood. 'I learned to read the poets, Latin and
Greek', carols Pierre, with a tenor's light and lyrical ease: 'Fumus
tormentorum suorum', mutters Father Philippe, with the double-
basses carrying his notes down into the depths. Pierre's song becomes
more and more romantic as he tries to win Alison's sympathy by
describing how he has had to sell his books to get the next meal.
When he comes to 'with a grieving heart, I said "Then I must part
with mighty Homer's poem"', the over-acting runs riot, and the
music becomes almost identical with some of the most disastrous
lapses in Holst's 'Early Horrors'. There are sequences of Chopin-like

rising semiquaver passages landing up on a good old Wagnerian
C♯ E G B. The tenor's high A is held fortissimo, after which the full
orchestra, *colla voce*, moves voluptuously on to a second inversion
of A with an added F♯, underlining Pierre's appropriate gesture and
holding the outrageous platitude for an impressive length of time.
The sound fades on to E F♮ A C♮ ¹ F ¹ as Alison succumbs to the Scholar's
charms, completely won over by all those chromatic sequences. 'So
learnéd a clerk', she sighs, *senza misura*, 'and so comely!' Father
Philippe's protest is a brilliantly economical bit of characterization,
borrowed from the two quavers that marked his first appearance in
Ex. 71:

Ex. 72.

It leads to a typical fugal passage for Father Philippe's threatening
gestures; the two unrelated keys snap at each other across the bar-
line, and the bitonality grows angrier and more jarring as he chases
Pierre out of the door, brandishing a cudgel. As the story unfolds,
Father Philippe becomes increasingly ridiculous. 'Repent', he says
to Alison: 'repent, on my bosom.' The portentous rising minor sixth
with its pause on 'repent' gives way to the absurd staccato quavers of
the first bar of Ex. 72 for 'on my bosom'. 'The demon of Spring so
torments me today', replies Alison, quoting his rising quavers on G♭
and B♭, but andante and legato, the held D♮ F of the clarinets
banishing all the absurdity and bringing in its place a faint recollection of the torment of that 'insolent slave'. When she objects to
bolting the door in case her husband might return, Father Philippe
bursts into his crowning absurdity:

Ex. 73.

This is the sort of thing Holst had longed to be able to write in his
early days, when each attempt at high comedy had turned into little
more than imitation Sullivan. Now, in the years of his maturity, he
could toss it off without effort, relishing the flavour.

Not only had he learnt to assimilate parody: he had also learnt to hold the drama of a situation. As Alison tries to push fat Father Philippe up the rickety ladder, the descending staccato scales in fifteen-eight make it plain that he will never manage to reach the attic. 'And here's a rung that's missing too', he blurts out indignantly, his flat feet flapping ineffectually while the cellos and basses lunge out on a sudden forte. In the middle of his clumsy anxiety he hears the bassoons playing Louis's cheerful folk-song: there can be no mistaking it, the honest husband is on his way home. Father Philippe scuttles precipitously down the ladder while Alison hides the wine and the cake. The angular tune of Ex. 70 punctuates her anxiety as she attempts to bury Father Philippe out of sight under a heap of straw. As Louis gets nearer, she begins scrubbing the kitchen table with feverishly exaggerated vigour, the high tremolo tension of $D\sharp''E\natural''F\natural''$ giving a sharp edge to her guilty conscience, while Louis's tune, played forte at the 'peevish' level of the cellos, with the infliction of an unwanted $D\sharp$ in the key of A, adds to the growing panic. When Louis and Pierre have made their leisurely entry, Alison and the young scholar compete with each other in the formal courtesy of their greeting, pretending they have never met before; but during the formalities an underlying tremor runs through the harmonies. There is the clash of D major over $E\flat$ when Alison implores Louis to take Pierre into town for a meal, as she has nothing to eat in the house. Four bars later, when Pierre insists on telling them a story, there is an impact of G minor and $F\sharp$ which recalls Father Philippe's earlier suggestion that they should bolt the door. Pierre tells his tale in an easy-going four-four, breaking off at the end of every verse into matter-of-fact conversational speech to bring home the dramatic point of the story. This abrupt change to the spoken word is extraordinarily effective: in *The Perfect Fool* Holst's ill-judged attempts to switch from song to speech and back again were exceedingly painful, but here he is on sure ground, and the drama moves freely. Louis can be equally dramatic: 'Pork! you say! *Pork?*' he exclaims incredulously, to the angular tune of Ex. 70. Then, as he lifts the lid of the casserole his astonishment slows the tune down until it becomes an *ad libitum* unaccompanied mutter of 'Well, is that pork or is it not?' The Scholar continues his story, while Alison's anxiety increases with the growing excitement of the counterpoint. Pierre's conventional tune changes to staccato diminution as it leads to the discovery of the cake. When he points out where the bottle of wine is hidden, wood-wind, horn, and strings burst into a fortissimo canon as Alison becomes more and more hysterical. The final disclosure, when Louis drags the quaking Father Philippe from under the heap of straw, is brief, comical, and very much to the point. Horns bellow their octave A while bassoons answer them in a protesting rising fifth of E♭ to B♭.

When Father Philippe has been kicked out, every ounce of excitement oozes out of the music. Louis sits down wearily to his supper, while an andante version of the angular tune in canon, a minor ninth apart, sums up the complicated emotional situation. The curtain falls as Louis drives Alison supperless to the attic. It is an abrupt end, but it is exactly in keeping with the way Holst's mind worked. He invariably avoided padding, and his final flourishes are often in the nature of a deliberate anticlimax. As soon as he had made his point, he stopped. These last fifteen bars tax the ingenuity of the producer very severely: each movement must be as economical as the music. The opera was performed during the last three months of Holst's life, but he was too ill to go and hear it. It is possible that he might have lengthened several of his phrases and fattened up some of his two-part counterpoint, in answer to the requests of his friends. He has pencilled in half a dozen queries in the manuscript score, and the words 'More?', 'More harmony?', 'Longer?', 'More space for movement?', appear several times in his handwriting. He was a practical man and he had the greatest respect for his colleagues. But it is doubtful if he would have made any structural alterations, for he believed it was a mistake for a composer to be *too* adaptable.

CHAPTER XVII

THE CHORAL FANTASIA AND HAMMERSMITH

(1930)

NINETEEN-THIRTY was one of the best years for composing that Holst had ever known. He had a fair amount of leisure, and for the first time in his life it was not an enforced leisure resulting from the strain of overwork. He was able to go about much more, listening to new music and making new friends. Filled with a sense of well-being, he no longer dreaded the effort of concentration, but enjoyed bringing all his energy to the works he had been commissioned to write.

The *Choral Fantasia*, written for the Three Choirs Festival, is a setting of verses from Bridges's 'Ode to Music'. He had been feeling his way towards this music ever since his early Rig Veda hymn, *To the Unknown God*. The rising Phrygian scale with which the Fantasia opens is no longer bare and aloof: the organ plunges fortissimo into the phrase that is to convey the vision of man gazing on creation and finding it good:

Ex. 74.

The short cadenza stretches upwards and outwards until it arrives on a long-held second inversion of G over a pedal C♯. This was the chord that upset the critic of *The Observer* at the first performance in Gloucester cathedral in 1931. He complained that 'when Holst begins his new *Choral Fantasia* on a six-four of G and a C♯ below that, with an air of take it or leave it, one is inclined to leave it'. But there was no take it or leave it about the sound in Holst's mind. It held not only the pull between flesh and spirit but also the recognition of their reliance on each other. From this quivering discord the solo soprano draws out the words of the opening verse:

Man born of desire
Cometh out of the night,
A wand'ring spark of fire,
A lonely word of eternal thought
Echoing in chance and forgot.

The desolation of the falling augmented triad is answered by the emptiness of the silence surrounding that last line. Then the rising challenge of the trombones and trumpets is flung across an un-bridgeable gap. The shuddering rhythm of the timpani is a reminder of the convulsive drums in the *Dirge for two Veterans*, and the quiet tune that follows, played *ppp* on the 16 ft., knows something of the 'colossal and mysterious' loneliness of *Egdon Heath*. Into the solitude the sweeping line of the seven-four 'Rejoice, ye dead' brings a return to the mood of the Whitsun festivals. Although this hymn is far removed from the tragic intensity of the opening, it is essential to the work as a whole. The *Choral Fantasia* does not lie for ever beyond time and space: we need the unforbidding familiarity of the Whitsun tune for the assurance that 'your names, remembered day and night, Live on the lips of those who love you well'. The graciousness is never allowed to blur the clear-cut outlines of the music; avoiding the false security of a modal complaisance, it reaches a lyrical beauty:

Ex. 75.

Here at last, for the space of three bars, Holst manages to find the warmth he had been searching for ever since listening to that per-formance of the Schubert Quintet. He was to lose it again, in moments of weariness, during the few remaining years. But having once found it, he could shake off the horror of numbness and isolation. There was to be no more despair.

At the climax of 'to light the glooms of Time with deathless flames', the rising fifths of that earlier nightmare pursuit are lifted high up in triumph, as at the moment of the victorious 'Vexilla Regis' in *The Hymn of Jesus*. When the chorus sings: 'He seeth the sun, He calleth the stars by name', the writing shares some of the poised ecstasy of *The Hymn of Jesus*. It is achieved with far fewer resources. The counterpoint is simple, in spite of the apparent complexity of the discords when they are considered as vertical harmony, and the imagination behind each word is radiant with the sudden astonishment of recognition:

Ex. 76.

Won·ders of   land   and   sea

At 'He striveth to know, To unravel the Mind That veileth in horror', Holst cuts through all the intervening surfaces and reveals the core of his creative thought. His own struggles had shown him the meaning of this agony: 'He striveth to know' is stark with the unyielding persistence of early organum; the bare fourths carve their way over the dirge of the drums, pausing on the brink of the abyss at the tension of 'horror', before stretching out in perfectly balanced supplication at 'He wills to adore'.

When the 'colossal and mysterious' chant is sung in two-part canon, the counterpoint unfolds hidden harmonic possibilities:

Ex. 77.

These are the sounds he had already hinted at years ago in Ex 22, when he had been searching for a way out of the darkness, not yet aware of the distance that still lay in front of him. In the *Choral Fantasia* he is able to move forward with all the strength of his mature experience.

A disillusioned comment greets the sentence 'He maketh a law No ill shall be'. The assurance with which the singers come to rest on a perfect fifth is immediately contradicted by an ironical reminder of the convulsive drums as the timpani and pizzicato strings quote their dirge-like procession. But the music is not allowed to finish on a note of disillusion. Nor does it die away with the desolate mutter of 'lost for aye with the things that are not'. A return to the lyrical beauty of Ex. 75 banishes all bitterness, making it possible for the soprano to end the work with the untroubled tranquillity of 'Rejoice ye dead, where'er your spirits dwell'.

It was during this same year that he wrote *Hammersmith*, a Prelude and Scherzo originally commissioned for military band, which he afterwards transcribed for full orchestra. The mood out of which the music had grown was a mood that had haunted him for nearly forty years: during his solitary walks in Hammersmith he had always been aware of the aloofness of the quiet river, unhurried and unconcerned, while just round the corner there was all the noise and hustle and exuberant vulgarity of the cockney crowd, pushing and shoving and sweating and swearing and shrieking and guffawing its good-humoured way. The river Prelude is founded on a ground bass:

Ex. 78.

During the sixty bars of its length the double-basses carry the rise and fall of these *pp* legato minims in F♯ minor, flowing as smoothly and deeply and unconcernedly as the river itself. When the bassoons enter with their tune in F major, there is no pull of opposing forces: nothing but a series of peaceful intervals, each voice blending with the other in one flowing stream of sound.

As the Prelude unfolds, he subtly changes the colours of his heavily laden stream, the flute in its lowest octave taking over from the bassoons. Suddenly the piccolo breaks into an impertinent whistle of greeting:

Ex. 79.

Trombones answer it from across the river with a quiet held triad of F major which moves up to G♭ major and subsides with an unobtrusive glissando back on to F; it is a sound that brings with it the discomfort of the fog and the unforgettable dank river-smell of the Thames. The diminuendo has scarcely died away before the solo trumpet, with 'coarse tone', blurts out Ex. 79. The ostinato dissolves into rising fifths, F♯ to C♯ alternating with D♮ to A♮ in a question-mark of suspense which leads to the opening of the Scherzo. The fugal subject is a typical Holst tune, with its silent first beats and its flick of a rising staccato fourth turned upside-down and brought scuttling back again a semitone lower (see facsimile). But unlike some of his cleverly contrived time-patterns, it has a rhythmic life of its own: there is a dancing response in the rise and fall of its tune. He very nearly wrecked its chances by putting accents over the quavers which happen on the beats of the bar. A note in his handwriting at the beginning of the flutes' first entry says: 'The accents must not be overdone.' But there was no need for them to be there at all.

The fugue is worked out with all his accustomed ingenuity: the dancing two-four is combined with a six-eight, and the countersubject is economically founded on the wriggling semiquavers at the end of the main tune. These semiquavers are carried along in a continuous stream, right-side-up and upside-down, forming a series of diminished fifths and minor sevenths and travelling chromatically

A PAGE FROM *HAMMERSMITH*

downhill until they arrive at a raucous tune (see bar 4 of facsimile) which is hurled to and fro before being grabbed by the solo tuba, where it finds a voice that suits it admirably. The passage that follows is a good example of the neat economy of his leggiero contrapuntal writing; the flute has the fugal subject beginning on D♮, the English horn and viola quarrel over it in close stretto on A♭, while the bassoon has a characteristic rising scale in semiquavers, beginning in C major and running into E major, which is taken over by the clarinet and transformed into the wriggling counter-subject shakes. Snatches of the river Prelude are heard through the fugue: a rising staccato C♯ to G♯ is answered by a rising A to E, bringing a disquieting recollection of those flowing fifths just before the beginning of the Scherzo. As the excitement mounts, the trombones plunge on to a series of consecutive second inversions and are joined by a crude and clamorous flourish on the solo trumpet, a flourish which might have been made by one or other of those tiresome Wizards. But here the boisterous vulgarity has come into its own. These are flesh and blood revellers who are shouting at each other: the raucous tunes whistling through the air sound far happier at a Saturday-night celebration in the Hammersmith Broadway than they ever sounded when they were laboriously spelt out by those hollow, arrogant sorcerers. The riot grows still livelier when the horns and trombones insist on holding their squashy discords, while the strings play the six-eight counter-subject with vigorous abandon, starting off in D and occasionally slipping into E♭ and having to jerk themselves back again. It is a cheerful and shockingly vulgar sound, leading, inevitably, to the first subject in augmentation; fortissimo, and ponderous with a drunken solemnity.

There is a howl of protest on a rising minor ninth which is repeated to form the ostinato bass for the tune of Ex. 79 on the three trumpets in unison; the wood-wind, determined not to be outdone, borrowing the last six quavers and making an episode of them, an augmented fifth apart. Owing to the shape and nature of the tune and its strained relations with the ostinato bass, this unhappy interval acquires a more devastating and cacophonous sound than it normally possesses. By the time the subject in augmentation has combined forces with Ex. 79 the climax is not far off. It arrives with a head-on collision. When the fury has worn itself out from sheer exhaustion, we are allowed the relief of a lyrical section where the English horn plays the six-eight counter-subject in a legato *con espress.* three-four, with the violins' and violas' quietly held major sevenths resolving on to minor sevenths and floating chromatically downstream in ghostly imitation of the trombones' fog-signal glissandos. The intense sadness of this passage is reminiscent of the Lament in the *Double Concerto*. Its brief fourteen bars of beauty are interrupted by the sounds of the last revellers tottering home: the pizzicato double-basses make a discreet attempt to close the door on the fugal subject, followed by the bassoon, who yawns his way into oblivion without waiting for the quaver rest at the beginning of his tune. Then at last the river is quiet, and there is a return to the mood of the Prelude in a slow, sad tune like a Nocturne:

Ex. 80.

Wisps of sound from the remembered revels scatter across the quiet spaces: wood-wind and horns join the Nocturne, the implied dominant seventh of their entry turning to plaintive resignation. All too soon we are brought back to the recapitulation of the Scherzo, where the intricate counterpoint has to deal with the added complication of having Ex. 79 wedged between subject and counter-subject, over a pizzicato echo of the Nocturne's falling semitone. The fugue unwinds itself with all its former excitement, reaching the orgy of a long semi-quaver passage where strings and wood-wind surge up and down in major sevenths and augmented fourths over the bellowing minor ninths of the tuba. Suddenly the uproar is completely blotted out. Nothing can be heard but the quiet flowing of the river Prelude. A few fragments of the Scherzo are tossed lightly to and fro, but their whispers become long-drawn-out with weariness. Soon they melt into a cantabile and dissolve into the deep peace of the Prelude's opening tune. Quietest of all are the last eighteen bars of molto adagio where, over the river's ostinato, the muted strings float their way through the Nocturne of Ex. 80. Muted trumpet and trombone are heard echoing the last sinking semitones, and then it is left to the strings to draw the quiet waves of sound into silence.

Here, in the middle of an over-crowded London, Holst had dis-covered the same tranquillity that he had found in the solitude of Egdon Heath.

CHAPTER XVIII

WELSH FOLK-SONGS AND THE MALE-VOICE CHORUSES

(1930–2)

AFTER writing *Hammersmith*, it was almost against his will that he began setting the *Twelve Welsh Folk-Songs* for unaccompanied voices. He felt he had done enough folk-song arrangements for one lifetime. But the tunes tempted him, and when Steuart Wilson had written free translations that fitted the tunes as if they had grown up with them, Holst set to work and enjoyed himself. As usual, it was just the right thing for him at the right moment. Twenty-five years before this, in the painful struggles of apprenticeship, he had needed the economy of folk-songs to free him from an overdose of chromatic romanticism. Now, at the end of his life, their simplicity helped to save him from an overdose of intellectual counterpoint.

The *Welsh Folk-Songs* are more economical than any of his earlier settings. The voices move stepwise within the mode, disclosing hidden treasures in the tunes and providing occasional pungent discords whenever they are wanted. In *The Mother-in-law* he hints at the old woman's cackling screeches by leaping on to sevenths and ninths, but it is always the tune that does the leaping: the alto and baritone spend most of their time bumping up against it in consecutive thirds before trailing off into their lilting and lackadaisical chorus of 'mouth-music'.

In feeling his way towards his new freedom, he was no longer scared of 'ordinary' harmonies. In *The Nightingale and the Linnet* nineteenth-century cadences put in an unabashed appearance from time to time and sound perfectly in keeping with his own way of thought. The many subtle touches of characterization prevent these cadences from becoming solid or four-square; in *Green Grass* he brings out the would-be jauntiness of 'don't believe my heart is breaking' by a clever mixture of a suggested swagger in the persistent crotchets and of an underlying melancholy in the minor sevenths. The consecutive fifths that float their way through *The Dove* are in a different world from the spineless drifting of some of his 1908 settings: they have a tenderness that is aware of the torment of augmented and diminished intervals, and they are utterly free from any trace of neo-modal snobbishness.

K

It was also partly against his will that he wrote his last two piano pieces. The *Nocturne* was an answer to a request for a piano solo without any folk-tunes in it. Whenever he heard it played, he got the impression that it had been written by someone else. It was not that he actively disliked it, but he found it difficult to believe that he had ever brought himself to the point of writing such music. Yet the cold, silvery enchantment of the opening is unmistakable, with its rising fifths and its trickling semiquavers remoulding the shape of their phrase until they have worn away the hard edges of the four beats in a bar. The piece is somewhat scattered and disjointed, but it has its moments of magic.

The *Jig* for piano, written two years later than the *Nocturne*, is chiefly interesting as a rehearsal for the *Scherzo* from the unfinished symphony. Apart from a short interlude of legato broken chords, most of the writing in the *Jig* is more like a short score of an orchestral piece than a work intended for piano. The fragmentary trumpet-call, flung a semitone higher with a reckless disregard for the pulse of the six-eight, is saved from too painful a jerkiness by the even-flowing counter-subject which links the two conflicting challenges and carries them along the stream:

Ex. 81.

Not content with the cross-rhythm of the three crotchets in the six-eight bar, he joins them into two-bar phrases and gives an impression of three-two against twelve-eight, as in *Mercury*. A variant of the counter-subject, in an implied nine-eight, begins with some of the mildness of *The Morning of the Year*, but soon encourages one of those jog-trot whole-tone scales the Wizards used to indulge in. At the end there is a characteristic *senza misura*, where the quiet arpeggio flows into the hush of a long-held pause before the boisterous jog-trot tune breaks the spell and slams down its parting expletive.

It was while he was teaching in America during the early months of 1932 that he was asked to write a serious work for jazz orchestra.

The 'jazz band piece' was never performed, and was later discarded. It has flashes of his mature thought and feeling, but on the whole it is a patch-work affair, concocted from several clever, characteristic utterances, and strung together with his usual deftness of orchestration. The opening quasi-folk-song for viola sounds as if it might almost belong to the *Country Song*, and the resemblance grows stronger as the sweeping rise of the harp's cadenza invites the strings to play it in three octaves over quiet sustained chords from the brass. But the mood soon changes when the tune breaks off for an animated fragment of conversation between a couple of saxophones and the marimba:

Ex.82.

These casual remarks turn into a three-part fugue in which the tuba firmly plants one flat foot after another in grotesque imitation of the capers in a morris jig. Later, a typical brass-band passage slithers chromatically off its beaten track:

Ex.83.

It seems at first to have little connexion with Holst's aloof austerity, but the humour is unforced, and it has learnt an added exuberance from the Saturday-night tunes in *Hammersmith*. So has the scherzando version of the conventional um-cha um-cha:

Ex.84.

With the return of the imitation folk-tune we are given chimes of descending quavers in fourths, phrased across the bar-line, on wood-wind, piano and Glockenspiel, over held pedal notes on the brass. The music is back again in the world of 1908, where it is content to manufacture a climax out of pleasant-sounding safe assertions. Small wonder that the tuba protests, breaking rudely into a pesante version of the tune in Ex. 84. Marimba and saxophone take advantage of the interruption, and continue their animated conversation of Ex. 82, the contrapuntal threads being drawn swiftly and neatly together in a coda where every note is packed with the precision of his own dry humour.

This same humour can be heard in the *Drinking Song*, one of his male-voice settings of Helen Waddell's Mediæval Latin Lyrics, where he obviously enjoys the rare luxury of having a guitar-like accompaniment. 'No room among the happy For modesty' says the poet, and Holst cheerfully acquiesces, tasting to the last drop the unexpected flavour of the wry discord. There is a suggestion of infinite scorn in the isolated word 'sobriety': the muttered unison, banished to a low level almost out of the tenors' reach, has the effect of transforming this harmless, necessary virtue into a shocking indiscretion. The timing and inflection are superb. They give such a startlingly clear glimpse of Holst himself that one can almost hear his pained tone of voice and see his face lengthening in mock horror, after an apprehensive pursing of the lips in the semiquaver rest.

In Helen Waddell's translations he found the right meeting-place for mellowness and austerity: the words had a concentrated symmetry that matched his own directness of thought, and their beauty helped to lead him still farther out of reach of the desolation which had been closing in on him. Not that there is any sudden access of warmth in these choruses for male voices and strings. *A Love Song*, one of the two-part canons for tenor and bass, appears to be as meagre and haggard as ever. There are no nightingales in this lyric; it is a sharp protest of pain that cuts through the silence:

> Noblest, I pray thee,
> Have pity upon me,
> Thy face is a sword,
> And behold, I am slain.

The pizzicato strings are merciless as they repeat their four-four crotchets, their separate and inaccessible beats becoming more and more insistent as the singers mount to their climax of 'Aid, oh aid!' The quiet three-four meno mosso at 'Love the deceiver' is never allowed to relax into the lilt of a serenade: the pizzicato has still got a hard edge to it, and the thin high mosquito-note of the first violins drives the nerves still farther towards their breaking-point. At the end there is dramatic intensity in the sudden emergence of all the arco strings as they bear down heavily on their repeated discord, until the short silence brings the loosening of the tension on a long-drawn-out pause of an unsatisfied second inversion.

Before Sleep holds something of the grey tranquillity of the river in *Hammersmith* as its canon unfolds in the smooth stream of sound. The tenors sing their descending scale in A minor and the basses in F minor, their two keys flowing into one over the low held pedal E. Sometimes the E is a dominant pedal, with the A♭ implying a G♯: sometimes the held E becomes a leading-note, with the tenors' C melting into the F minor of the basses. This effortless fluctuation is typical of his polytonal writing: although the key-signatures may seem to contradict each other on paper, the music never loses its clear tonality. In the last verse of *Before Sleep*, the quiet canon achieves a rarer tranquillity than the ending of *Hammersmith*, where the river spread outwards and flowed on: here the soothing hush flows inwards, filling the small space in the tired brain.

In *How mighty are the Sabbaths*, the longest of the male-voice choruses, the majestic seven-four must have reminded him of the first Whitsun festival at Thaxted: inevitably the hymn belongs to the

familiar world of amateur music-making. But in *Intercession* and
Good Friday he enters the next stage of his journey beyond the *Choral
Fantasia*. The severe lament of *Intercession* moves over the even
crotchets of a ground bass which alternates between 2+3 and 3+2.
Critics have often complained of Holst's persistent use of this particular time-pattern, but it was the necessity of satisfying his inner ear
in its search for the musical idiom of the English language which led
him again and again to this andante five-four. The rhythm must have
been crying out to him from the very first moment when he read the
words:

> Set free Thy people, set free Thy servants, . . .
> Look on their anguish, bitter their weeping,
> Christ, in Thy mercy.

The stress on the second 'free' adds weight to the urgency of its
repetition, and the pause on 'anguish' suggests an agony that clutches
at the throat and remains poised in the vulnerable 'ng'. The harmonies, being an inseparable part of the rhythm, pull on the tension
of 'bitter' and gradually release it as they rise chromatically to the
relaxation of the first inversion on 'weeping'. Each harmonic change
is brought about by the words; the moment of coming to rest on the
E major chord at the end of the long-drawn-out 'mercy' shares the
mood of a Kyrie that knows it is already absolved, but there is no
feeling of absolution in the anxious litany at 'Spare us we pray Thee':
here the phrase falls instead of spreading outwards, and the E minor
chord is weighed down by oppression. The anxiety deepens at 'Thy
merited wrath', where the D$\sharp_1$ over B$\natural_{11}$ changes to E$\flat_1$ over C$\natural_{111}$.
Perhaps it is the enormous drop of an extended major seventh that
brings such a sense of doom to this enharmonic change. It is a change
that needs the flexible adjustment of the voices and strings: there is
a distinct difference of pitch between the D$\sharp$ and the E$\flat$, and the
arrival on C minor suffers from the fixed temperament of the piano
or organ.

Good Friday is the last of all those sad processions that had moved
through his mind for over thirty years. It is a setting of Abelard's
'Alone to sacrifice Thou goest, Lord'. The writing is as economical
as in *Turn Back O Man*: the voices chant smoothly above the descending crotchets of the ostinato tonic-dominant-tonic, the basses singing
for most of the time in stepwise consecutive thirds. But this simplicity
reaches an intense fervour that is only equalled in the greatest
moments of the *Choral Fantasia*. When the pattern of the ground
bass changes and the falling fourth becomes augmented, it darkens

the whole line of the hymn, bringing a passionate pleading to the unfulfilled dominant minor ninth on the word 'Lord'. There is also intensity in the sorrowful stress on 'our deeds, our deeds', as the rising augmented fourth changes enharmonically to a diminished fifth, implying a second inversion of the dominant chord.

At long last Holst had learnt to overcome his distrust of dominant sevenths. Having broken away from the deceiving self-sufficiency of neo-modal flattened sevenths, he now felt an overwhelming desire for the tenderness he had denied himself in the bleak discomfort and restlessness of the years when he had been writing all those staccato major sevenths. The search for warmth had led him, by hard and laborious ways, back to the dominant sevenths he had been trying to escape from most of his life. There was no longer any need to confine his augmented fourths and diminished fifths to the empty, cold desolation of the opening of *Saturn*. He could now let them share in the expectancy and longing they bring to music of any generation, whether it is written by Schubert or by Pérotin. This was a freedom he had at last won for himself, and, indirectly, for others who were to come after him.

CHAPTER XIX

THE LYRIC MOVEMENT AND THE UNFINISHED SYMPHONY

(1932–4)

HELEN WADDELL'S translations of Latin poems were still haunting him during the summer of 1932. He had apparently recovered from a severe illness in America, and as soon as he got back to England he began work on another eight lyrics, setting them as canons for equal voices. He had seldom reached such a rare enchantment as in *Evening on the Moselle*, where he draws out every particle of magic from those six short lines:

> What colour are they now, thy quiet waters?
> The evening star has brought the evening light,
> And fill'd the river with the green hill-side;
> The hill-tops waver in the rippling water,
> Trembles the absent vine and swells the grape
> In thy clear crystal.

The tune alone, sung unaccompanied, contains the essence of the lyric: when its E minor is answered in C minor and linked by the merging waves of sound in the accompaniment, the magic deepens. The clear light of the river and the clear taste of the wine are both tinged with the cloud of exile, and Holst suggests this subtle transformation by seeming to drift chromatically in thirds while actually keeping to the clear outlines of diatonic contrary motion:

Ex. 85.

Everything is there: the quiet of the opening question; the colours that flow into each other; the to and fro of the quavers as the hill-tops waver in the rippling water, meeting and dividing at the quiver of the semitone; and the clearing of the reflection, when the water is so still that each detail becomes sharp-edged in the memory. Technically he achieves this blend of simplicity and enchantment by linking the separate keys of the voices with the shared notes of their accompaniment. He uses the same device in *If 'twere the time of lilies,* where the F minor tune is echoed a bar later in B minor, the two keys being stitched together by the piano's dry staccato fifths until they meet in an undisputed F major. Heard without the accompaniment, the two voices sound incurably unhappy, but the pin-pricks of the mutually related fifths help to disperse the melancholy.

In the unaccompanied canons it was much more difficult to prevent the polytonal counterpoint from splintering into a sparse dejection. He had to trust his singers to give and take with ungrudging generosity. The strained relationship of E minor, C minor, and A♭ minor suits the melancholy of *Lovely Venus*: there is an echo of the sad cadence of the Bridges *Elegy* at 'violets wither'. The harmonic progressions are simple, but the harmonies are only implied, for he seldom asks for an enharmonic change. Each voice sings a minor key of its own and hopes for the best, instinctively spreading the inequality over each phrase to avoid the shock of meeting on a too-hastily adjusted 'unison' between D♯ and E♭ or between A♯ and B♭. The canon is not difficult to sing once the tune has been learnt by heart: the only difficulty is in sight-reading, when an over-intelligent interest in the vertical appearance of the score is apt to lead to disaster. This also applies to *The Fields of Sorrow*. Here he is once more in the desolate regions of the Prelude to the *Choral Symphony*:

> They wander in deep woods, in mournful light,
> Amid long reeds and drowsy-headed poppies
> And lakes where no wave laps. . . .

The shape of the tune reveals the awareness of one who has long been familiar with these particular fields. The drowsy-headed poppies lean over: the texture of that semiquaver drop of an octave is so fragile that one can almost hear the petals fall. There is a morendo hush for the voiceless streams, and a chromatic groping for the dim light that drains the colour from the withering flowers as the second inversion of D♯ major fades to D♯ minor. It is this descent from major to minor that expresses the grief of *David's Lament for Jonathan*: the sinking semitones at 'Low in thy grave with thee' become laden with sorrow as each voice enters and drags the harmonies down, resignedly transforming the major triads into minor triads, until the grief mellows with acquaintance and moves towards a diatonic cadence in answer to its own question.

Where the words are not 'over-sadly tinged', he avoids conflicting key-signatures. The allegretto A minor and E minor of *If you love songs* slips easily through one unrelated triad after another, with time to savour the sadness of 'Alcuin the old man thinks long for thee', as the sudden B minor darkens the line between the A♭ major of 'Spring is here' and the still brighter A major of the 'green meadows'. It is the tune itself that brings about these frequent changes, without ever disturbing the simplicity of its seventeen bars. And in *Truth of all Truth*, the harmonic possibilities are already suggested in the single line of the tune: its shape is so completely satisfying that the ear can follow its course through the six voices and the three keys, welcoming the descent of the overlapping quavers as they flow through the music at each repetition of the word 'Holy'. There is no perilous anxiety about this counterpoint: it is freed from the burden of its own cleverness and can move with ease and grace.

He had now reached the stage in his technique when there was no longer any need to struggle. In his next work, the *Lyric Movement* for viola and small orchestra, the music reaches sustained warmth. He wrote it at a time when he was physically weakened by illness. But in spite of the pain and the restricted life and the exasperation of keeping to a diet of milk, he found he had energy for writing. And he could recognize his new-found strength. When I told him how much I liked the *Lyric Movement* he said: 'Yes, it looks as though I'll have to go on being an invalid if I'm going to write music like that.'

There is no sudden change of style in the work. Some of the ideas which had persistently followed him throughout his life are brought together again, finding themselves thoroughly at home in the new warmth and vitality of this short movement. The opening *senza misura* for solo viola begins with rising fifths, but they are not his usual hushed *senza espress.* fifths, drifting upwards out of silence until they float beyond time and space, to be lost and received in the silence from which they emerged. These fifths are passionate. Growing from a reverberating low D, they rise with zest, exulting in an overflowing strength that spills itself in a cascade of falling semiquavers. The first tune, founded on a fragment of the opening cadenza, moves through characteristic syncopation and repetition in quicker time-values, but there is nothing disjointed in the sound of this familiar device; a warm tone breathes through the legato phrase, lending grace to each leaning gesture. When the soloist quotes the second tune in passionate augmentation, the sforzando fourth breaking in on it is the same framework that once surrounded the sad recitative in the Bridges *Elegy*: here, it turns aside from the melancholy of resignation and sounds a challenge that unconsciously travels back nearly forty years to the time when he had first heard Tristan and had waited in an agony of suspense for the arrival of the C♯ in the forty-fourth bar of the Prelude. The *Lyric Movement* is as far removed from Tristan as it could possibly be, but in it Holst recaptures the ardour which had possessed him at the very beginning of his creative life, an ardour he had rejected during the long years when he was working out his own salvation.

There are many moments of sensuous beauty in the work, but every phrase has been severely pruned. A murmuring semiquaver passage for flute and clarinet brings a lyrical recollection of the fifteen-eight counterpoint in *Egdon Heath*: the murmur has lost all the bare, exposed discomfort of Ex. 65, but its outline is just as clear-cut. Even when the strings transform the semiquavers into surging waves, the sound remains clear. The tender austerity of the poco adagio fulfils the promise of warmth that was first heard in the *Choral Fantasia*:

Ex. 86.

It is a return to the voice of Savitri at her most inspired moments. But it was not a deliberate return to an earlier freedom, nor was it chance that had led him there; it was the accumulated experience of a lifetime of struggle, experiment, failure, and isolation. He had earned this beauty, and now that he had found it, he knew how to hold it in security.

The end of the work gives a glimpse of what the slow movement of his symphony might have been like, if he had lived to write it.

Throughout 1933 he was having to spend a good deal of his time in hospital. But there were very few weeks when he was not able to go on with his composing, and it was during this year that he wrote the

Brook Green Suite for strings, for the junior orchestra at St. Paul's Girls' School. The three short movements express his own contemporary thought in a language that can be understood by beginners in an amateur orchestra. The Prelude is founded on the descending scale of C, and the cellos are given the enormous satisfaction of carrying it right through two octaves and landing it on their open C string, over and over again. The *espressivo* passage breathes the melancholy of 'violets wither' in *Lovely Venus*, and the sweeping changes from C major to B major and from E minor to C minor bring a passionate intensity to the music. In the slow *Air* the flowing descants are reminiscent of the Welsh folk-song settings: perhaps it was these songs that helped him to write such tender harmonies at the change from E major to F minor. This change is characteristic of many of his polytonal works, but here the writing is simple enough for inexperienced players to follow the line of thought even when they are anxiously listening to their intonation. Later there is another example of how he bridges the gulf between the two halves of his 'double' life: the floating quavers in sinking semitones belong to the world of the *Choral Fantasia*, but here they have shed their dark remoteness and have come within the horizon of a school orchestra. In the last movement, a Jig with a cheerful tune he had once heard played in Sicily, there is a dramatic moment when the firsts hold their G^1 over the violas' and seconds' pause on A♭ and C^1. It is a sound that stretches towards the unfettered thought of 'open wide the mind's cage door', and he would have agreed with the white-haired gardener who was heard to explain, viola in hand, that 'you need to lean on that A♭ to get the full flavour of it'.

As usual, Holst was unconscious of the fact that he was bridging a gulf, though he knew that elementary orchestras needed an occasional respite from their modulations into the dominant, just as brass bands had needed a change from their operatic selections. Perhaps he also realized that audiences needed to get acquainted with contemporary music by trying to learn to sing and play it. But, as he himself said, he had 'no conscious principle, no "ideal", no axe to grind'. St. Paul's Girls' School had been his home for nearly thirty years: it was fitting that he should follow his own thought and feeling when writing for its orchestra.

Few things could have been farther from his own inclination than having to provide music for a Hollywood pageant of the *Song of Solomon*. The work was never finished, and the surviving fragments show that his heart was not in it. Through the made-to-measure descending scales and the rows of triads in contrary motion, there is an occasional turn of phrase that is unmistakable, such as the alto recitative:

Ex. 87.

and the male voice chanting of a psalm:

Ex. 88.

But these are rare instances. His own thought was bound up with his new symphony.

The *Scherzo* was the only movement that he managed to write: he finished scoring it in bed during the last few weeks of his life. The ostinato bursts into one of his usual fragmentary remarks, interrupting the silence at each deliberate change of inflection:

L

Ex.89.

But the restlessness does not last long: instead of insisting on a new stress at each repetition, he is content to let his quavers run on with the continuity of the fifth bar. The characteristic change of level helps him to move freely without losing his sense of stability. In his original sketch he wrote it in flats instead of sharps: the fourth note certainly feels more like an E♭ than a D♯, but there is no way of avoiding the unwanted diminished third, and the gap between G♭ and E♮ would have been just as clumsy as between F♮ and D♯.

From this ostinato the bassoons and clarinets emerge with their rising fourths:

Ex.90.

The relationship between these fourths had been clear and inevitable in Holst's mind for many years: sometimes, as at the end of *Egdon Heath*, the notes slowly stretch out into the remotest distance: here they are casual in their scherzando encounter.

When the trombones grasp a fragment of the ostinato and try to turn it into a tune, their efforts are at first clumsy and hesitant. But as soon as the flute borrows it, all its awkward edges are smoothed out in a flowing leggiero:

Ex.91.

Here at last is a fragmentary six-eight tune which is allowed to be free and graceful in its movements. Although the accents are still there to mark the beats, they no longer stab the rhythm, but warm it with the breath of their legato. Nor is there any longer a suggestion of an inaudible sniff halfway through each bar: the tune moves happily over the even pulse of the harp's chords, rejoicing in being able to dance through its rests. The trombones' glissando descent from the triad of A major to G♯ major brings a ghostly recollection of the river in *Hammersmith*: there is also a hint of those Saturday-night crowds in the clarinet's syncopated tune:

Ex.92.

On the surface it looks as though it is just one more example of his habit of calculating how to arrive on a different accent at each repetition. But this tune instinctively responds to the straight-forward encouragement of the bassoons and horns, instead of being tugged and twisted and turned inside out by a couple of over-intellectual counter-subjects with conflicting cross-rhythms of their own. The drawn-out syncopation in the third and fourth bars is perfectly balanced and suffers from none of the sprawling discomfort of his less fortunate dance tunes. Perhaps the 'jazz band piece' had helped to break down some of the barriers. Its influence can certainly be felt in the oboes' nonchalant six-fours in the second half of the tune:

Ex.93.

It is a sign of his new-found warmth that the slow cantabile five-four should be heard sempre *ff* from the passionate octaves of the strings, instead of in the remoteness of a restrained hush. When it eventually quietens and dissolves into ripples, the sensuous murmur remains clear in its outlines and is never allowed to become vague or nostalgic. The horn's legato solo has all the simplicity of the modal tunes he used to write for his amateurs, but there is nothing 'too easy' about this tune: it is inescapable and packed with meaning. The piercing wood-wind quavers move in and out with a tang that belongs to his own particular kind of espressivo. These are the same bitonal clashes he had often used in the past at moments of dazzling vision and emotional intensity: here the sounds are strung together in a haunting phrase that is sadly but not over-sadly tinged. While the last echoes of the cantabile tune are still hanging in the air, the ostinato creeps back again and works up to the height of its noise and bustle, breaking off characteristically for the solo violin's quiet contemplation, and ending with Holst's usual abrupt gesture of dismissal.

CHAPTER XX

THE END OF THE STRUGGLE AND THE BEGINNING OF THE RENAISSANCE

IT is useless to wonder what the other movements of the symphony would have been like: the few fragments of rough sketches are too short and disconnected to give any idea of the music that was in his mind. It would be just as useless to bewail the fact that he died before finishing the symphony. He had managed to solve his remaining problems. Today, thirty years after his death, this seems more important than the fact that he wrote very few works that are entirely satisfactory. Most of his life was spent in making mistakes which had got to be made. This was not only because of his own slow development: it was also because of the many upheavals in music during the first quarter öf the century, when composers had to unlearn most of what they had been taught in order to remain coherent. Holst had been born in 1874: it was inevitable that he should have become involved in these violent changes. He was able to help in the struggle owing to the strength of his imaginative vision: ever since hearing the Sanctus from the B minor Mass he had known what music was about. His vision had been so insistent that it had compelled him to avoid the snares of a pleasant English neo-modalism, just as it had compelled him to break through the layers of the nineteenth-century romanticism in which he had been nourished. His imagination was so piercing that it could reach out to old age in *Saturn* and could feel the sudden pain of being forced to look at the too-dazzling light in *The Hymn of Jesus*.

It was his imaginative attention to the smallest details of everyday life that helped to save him from wandering farther and farther into the remote distance. There can be no doubt about it that the remote distance was where he felt most at home. But his imagination never left him alone there: he was continually aware of the pursuing trumpets and the convulsive drums. Perhaps the height of his vision had been the realization that the emptiness of *Egdon Heath*, if it could only be accepted, would bring the final answer to the insistent trumpets and the sad procession.

Owing to the strength of his convictions it had been essential for him to learn to express himself with the utmost economy: he had fought his way out of lush extravagance and had begun his search for the musical idiom of the English language even before he had heard his first folk-song. Having no continuous tradition to help him, he had had to dig for his own materials. This directness was one of his chief characteristics; it led to his refusal to compromise, as well as to his lack of conventionality and his horror of repeating a success.

It was not only the strength of his writing that helped him to find his way through the difficult years of upheaval: his weaknesses also taught him a great deal about music. Possibly his two worst failings were an over-intellectual approach and a naïve obstinacy. Too much abstract thought had driven him into a dry desert. It had also hindered him from writing in extended form. The shape and purpose of his music depended on the inspiration of a mood that had been clearly imagined and deeply felt, as in *Saturn* or *Egdon Heath*. By cutting out the domestic emotions and trying to attack his problems with the attitude of mind of a mathematician he had crippled his chances of writing a symphony or a string quartet, where the form would have depended for its very existence on his being able to balance thought with feeling. Except where the mood was remote, and therefore his own, he had had to rely on words or a story for the structure of his music.

Some of the faults of his over-intellectual approach helped him, in a roundabout way, to work out his own salvation. The dry desert occasionally became so arid that it was obvious, even to his austere habit of mind, that something had got to be done about it. If the fourths in *The Perfect Fool* had not been so brittle and unreal, the Verdi Troubadour would not have challenged him to find a lyrical beauty of his own.

His other chief failing, his naïve obstinacy, also had its advantages. It meant that he insisted on making his own mistakes in his own way. And this was decidedly a blessing, for he would never have learnt so much if he had not written so many failures.

Being obstinate, he never wavered from his distrust of theoretical knowledge. 'I like everything—form, melody, harmony, etc.—to grow out of the original inspiration,' he once wrote. Even the search for the musical idiom of the English language had been an unconscious process until he reached the stage where he found that his words and his music were 'really growing together'. Analysis he considered 'quite interesting and not dangerous as long as you do not imagine that it has any direct bearing on Art'. Criticism he welcomed at all times; he used to say 'a sympathetic critic's disapproval is one of the most stimulating experiences I know'. And he believed that the critical faculty was just as necessary and important as the imaginative one. But he had little use for most critical text-books, and he had no patience whatsoever with 'learning for learning's sake'.

Having no theories about composition, he was seldom aware of any of the contemporary influences in his own music. He knew that he had been influenced by Vaughan Williams; from their first meeting in 1895 to the time of Holst's death in 1934 they had always shown each other the first rough drafts of their latest compositions. As a result of this close companionship it is not always easy to decide if Vaughan Williams has influenced Holst or if Holst has influenced Vaughan Williams: the dates of their publications are nothing to go by. Each of them used to declare, with the utmost sincerity, that he had borrowed extensively from the other. This mutual influence was strongest in 1905, when the folk-song revival completely changed Holst's way of thinking. It can also be detected in the layers of bitonal block counterpoint in Vaughan Williams's Pastoral Symphony. But after Holst had written his *Choral Symphony* their ways divided, and there is little of Vaughan Williams to be heard in Holst's later compositions, apart from superficial likenesses in some of the short neo-modal works and a passing reference to Job in the *Choral Fantasia*.

Possibly the most significant contemporary influence in his life was the effect that Stravinsky had on his music in 1914. Technically, it is immediately recognizable in the insistence of repeated time-patterns and the bitonal clashes of C to F$\sharp$. This relationship between C and F$\sharp$, however, and between C and D$\flat$, can hardly be considered as a local or a personal influence; throughout Europe composers were seizing hold of these sounds in their conscious or unconscious attempts to get away from the clearly defined major and minor keys that music had relied on for over two hundred years. In his persistent use of the interchange between C and D$\flat$, Holst was helping to disperse the deep-rooted associations of the dominant seventh, a painful but necessary procedure in the early years of the century. It was his great good fortune that he just had time to return home again to the sound of the dominant seventh, by his own devious and uncomfortable route.

Apart from the help Stravinsky had given him, the other influences in 1914 were only slight and temporary. When people complain that *The Planets* is 'full of quotations' they sometimes forget that many of these quotations are film and radio borrowings dating from after the first performance of the work. Holst himself resisted the temptation to repeat the easy success of the most highly coloured pictorial effects in *The Planets*, but there are other composers who have gone on quoting indispensable snippets ever since, until the work has been in danger of turning into a communal storehouse of clichés.

Holst's dislike of theoretical knowledge was bound to lead to a certain loss of self-criticism. But in some ways it was helpful, especially in the 'tomorrow I may do something quite different' attitude. And it prevented a hardening process from setting in. His fondness for three keys had grown from the actual sounds they made; being unconcerned with their paper-work possibilities, he was saved from the delusion of systematized counterpoint.

Another sign of his obstinacy was the way he insisted on spending most of his time and energy on teaching. His friends tried to warn him of the damaging effect that the strain of overwork was having on his music, but he enjoyed working with amateurs so much that he refused to listen to their advice. Even his weariness, however, was sometimes a blessing in disguise. In the years when he was so tired that he dreaded the effort of concentration, he had not been able to find enough warmth or vitality for the shortest and simplest of his works for amateurs. This meant that he had had to get right down to the root of the trouble. If he had always found the necessary warmth in his Whitsun hymns and dances, it might have kept his two 'lives' entirely separate. And this would probably have meant that he would have remained cold and dry and solitary in his own thought, instead of struggling towards the freedom of the *Lyric Movement*. His last works owe some of their greatness to the fact that in the end he managed to break down all the remaining barriers between the two different worlds in which he lived.

There is no doubt that his weariness meant a loss to music. But it is impossible to measure this loss against the importance of his achievements in bridging the gulf between the composer and the listener and in helping to put an end to the false distinction between music and contemporary music. This is something that cannot be thought of in terms of his own output: it means considering him, not as a separate individual, but as an essential part of the new music that was beginning to grow up during his lifetime. And this makes it seem comparatively unimportant whether many of his works written before the mid-nineteen-twenties will survive.

What is quite certain is that the fruits of his experience will survive. The lessons he learnt so painfully are now taken for granted, and the mistakes he made will never have to be made again.

Ever since leaving college, he had dreamed of the possibility of a renaissance of music in England. He died before he could be certain that it was going to happen. Without realizing it, he had been preparing the way for it with every note of his compositions. Some of the music that is being written today bears an unmistakable resemblance to the clarity of his mind and mood. Even when there is no actual resemblance in idiom or structure, the stream of his thought and experience has helped to bring it about. This is the only kind of immortality he would have chosen. He had no use for personal fame or success. But he cared a very great deal for the fellowship of 'those who carry musical souls about them'.

HOLST'S LECTURE AT YALE ON
THE TEACHING OF ART
1929

[In 1924 Holst was given the Howland Memorial Prize by Yale University, a medal awarded to 'a citizen of any country in recognition of some marked distinction in the field of literature or the fine arts'.]

AT last I have an opportunity of thanking this university for the honour she did me in presenting me with the Howland prize. This, in itself, was sufficient cause for gratitude. But this feeling of gratitude was rendered greater when I read the list of previous prize winners.

I felt then that I had received the greatest honour this world can give—the company of honourable men.

In talking of the Teaching of Art I shall chiefly use illustrations from my own art, music.

But I trust that most of what I have to say may be of interest to all of you as it applies to every kind of art, not only the 'Fine' ones, and to teaching in general.

Most people who have mastered any form of intellectual activity either are, have been, or are in danger of becoming teachers even for a short time.

It is a fate that few escape.

At the same time it is noticeable that the teacher is an object of derision amongst many writers of today.

He is held up as being too pedantic in trifles and, above all, too fond of giving good advice.

Personally I think this applies still more to the critics of teachers— people who have never done a day's teaching in their lives and therefore are able to criticize us more freely.

All the same it is often quite true of many of us.

It is true of me at this moment. I am going to indulge in advice-giving now.

I suggest that teachers should be good trades-unionists and in such matters as correcting others and giving good advice we should not work overtime without extra pay.

A second reason for our unpopularity is summed up in a saying of George Bernard Shaw:

'Those who can, do: those who can't, teach.'

As a mere statement of facts this is fairly accurate.

In the musical profession nearly everyone has to teach. The reason is an economic one—there is a larger demand for teachers than for singers and players.

That remark of Shaw is not *essentially* true.

Teaching is not an alternative to doing.

Teaching *is* doing. Teaching is an art.

'Those who can, do.' Those who teach also 'do'.

My subject today is this 'doing' in its relation to the training of artists.

In the teaching of art we aim at the production of artists, of exceptional people, of aristocrats, in whatever department of life they may happen to be, whether builders of cathedrals or good cooks in village inns.

The best definition of what I call an aristocrat is Gilbert Murray's: 'Every man who counts is a child of a tradition and a rebel from it.'

The production of such a man is the aim of the teaching of art.

If we are teachers our first duty is to make our pupil a child of a tradition.

We can only do that if we are ourselves its children. Not merely students but children, steeped in the love of our tradition—that unconscious love that children possess and which is the most contagious emotion in the world.

Our influence on our pupil is assured if we have this.

This influence will be first directed towards developing technical power in the pupil.

By technique I mean the means by which you express yourself.

And the method of acquiring technique is, for nearly all of us, Hard Work.

People like Mozart, in whom all necessary technique seems to have been born, are too rare to form the basis of an argument.

Of course ideas on hard work vary from time to time.

About a hundred years ago a father brought his six-year-old son to a famous violinist for advice.

The answer was something like this:

'If you want your son to become a violinist make him practise ten hours a day from now until he is twenty-one.'

Today, if a father tried such a plan on a six-year-old boy, he would probably find himself in the police court.

Nowadays the danger is in the other extreme.

In musical circles, a few years ago, we were told: 'We cannot make all our children good singers and players, therefore let us make them good listeners.'

I agree, on condition that we remember that the surest way of becoming a good listener is to first try and sing or play.

For those who are working at technique, some sort of what is called 'Musical Appreciation' is excellent. And in nearly every case the modern systematic system of teaching it is the best.

But I earnestly plead that in all cases it should be coupled with practical experience in making music.

And if there is not time for both theory and practice, let us have practice only.

Using the word in the non-technical sense, appreciation always accompanies genuine technical work, however slight, whether in music or in any other art.

Years ago I cycled with a friend to a famous cathedral.

On arrival I merely wandered about, vaguely trying to impress various details on my mind. My friend spent the whole day in sketching. The sketches were not remarkable and the artist had no illusions about them. But there was no doubt as to which of us two had best realized the beauty of the cathedral.

I have said that the first aim of the teacher should be to make the pupil a child of a tradition.

It must be a living tradition—one of great art and great men.

Such things as standard textbooks and technical exercises must never usurp the place of a living tradition.

But they must not be ignored even if their place be a lower one.

The practice of technical exercises and the learning of textbooks are short cuts.

As someone said the other day: 'The best technique is the laziest way of doing anything.'

It is the best means to an end.

Here, as everywhere else, we are sometimes apt to mistake the means for the end.

That is why I insisted that the teacher must be the child, and the loving child, of a tradition.

And now I am going to use a word that is so often misapplied that I must dwell on its real meaning for a moment.

That word is Stimulant.

To most of us it suggests whisky. But I have been assured on excellent authority that alcohol is not a real stimulant.

In order to be quite sure of my ground I consulted a doctor friend who kindly gave me the following definition.

'A Stimulant is an agent to arouse the nervous system to greater exhibition of energy.

'A true Stimulant imparts no power. It compels brain, muscle, or other part of the organism, to liberate stored-up energy.

'It is on account of this power to exhaust energy that a *large* dose of stimulant produces the same effect as a narcotic.

'It tends to produce narcotism or paralysis.'

As an example of a real Stimulant my friend mentioned Cold—something natural, inevitable to most of mankind, and moreover, something beneficial.

Bearing this in mind, I ask you to go through my friend's definition again, substituting the word 'Examination' for 'Stimulant'.

I would no more think of condemning examinations and competitions than I would think of condemning cold weather.

It would be almost as futile and quite as silly.

But, just as hard work was, in former generations, sometimes considered as an end in itself and not a means: just as today a few people dream glibly of substituting talking about art for making art and therefore bring the excellent idea of Musical Appreciation into contempt; so, occasionally, one comes upon a piano student whose idea of musical life is just one examination after another; or else a choir, the members of which have lost all feeling for music as music and are only interested in the number of marks they may or may not gain in their competition.

A feeling for music is inherent in nearly all of us, but in the vast majority it is a delicate plant and one that is easily crushed out of existence by that vigorous weed, pot-hunting.

Once again, it is only the over indulgence in this natural, inevitable and beneficial stimulant that is to be deplored.

The Competitive Musical Festivals have been some of the greatest boons in musical education in Great Britain—boons that are still increasing in virtue as well as in mere size.

In every Festival I have attended, the aim seemed to be music first and last. In most cases competitors have been animated by the same spirit.

The stimulation of occasional examinations or other tests and the short cuts in technical training are only two of the many tools which the teacher will use in order to fulfil the first part of Gilbert Murray's definition and make the pupil a child of a tradition.

The teacher being one already, there will grow up between them that beautiful comradeship which is the great reward of teaching.

We read of painters in former ages whose pupils actually worked in their masters' studios.

What a perfect way of learning art! Imagine the joy of watching a great master of painting at work: and the even greater joy of being allowed to finish a background for him!

But this comradeship of master and pupil has its dangers.

The teacher may consciously or unconsciously influence his pupil too much or for too long.

We must remember the last words in Gilbert Murray's dictum: 'Every man who counts is a child of a tradition and a rebel from it.'

The civilized world is crowded with buildings, pictures, poems, novels and musical compositions produced by children of various traditions who never grew to be rebels and who, therefore, do not 'count'.

If we, as teachers, force the characters of our pupils into a mould or allow them to drift there, we are not artists but experts in standardized mass-production.

I have been told that standardized mass-production is excellent for motor-cars: it is sometimes fairly effective for detective-stories. But it is iniquitous for human beings and impossible for art.

A true work of art is imbued with a vitality of its own.

This appears very clearly in the work of novelists and dramatists.

Over and over again writers have told us how their characters grow individualities of their own and often insist on behaving in a way their creator never intended.

A dramatist has assured us that he has no more control over the women in his plays than he has over his wife.

A novelist is said to have shed tears on discovering that his heroine was going to die.

This is being a creative artist—the creator of men and women who live their own lives.

And this should be the ideal of the teacher of art. It will be so if he is an artist in teaching.

A moment will come when he realizes that he has done his share in the work of creating a 'rebel' who will 'count'. The man who spent his life always retouching one picture instead of leaving it for another would not be a real artist but a more or less interesting study in morbid psychology.

The last and hardest duty of a teacher is to make himself unnecessary.

I have tried to prove to you that the teaching of art is, itself, an art.

Nearly everything I have said about the production of an artist would apply equally to the production of a good picture, poem, symphony, dance, dress, or dinner.

All must spring from a tradition and yet bring something fresh to the world if they are to be works of art.

So if 'those who can, do': those who teach also 'do'.

And in conclusion I would like to point out that those who 'do' usually teach as well.

The vast majority of the great artists of the world have been teachers—usually very good ones.

Of course they grumbled when too much time had to be spent in teaching or when their pupils were more stupid than usual. Who wouldn't?

But this is very different from despising teaching *qua* teaching.

By a happy coincidence the first thing I read on my arrival in Yale was an article by Harold Laski on 'The Academic Mind'. In writing about a certain type of fine thinkers he says 'They have to communicate the truth they have found because, like all great artists, they are born teachers; and silence for them, in the realm they deem supremely important, is worse than death.'

As opposed to these, there is the other type of artist who tries to live in a world by himself: one who despises the vulgar herd and only condescends to allow it to share the beauty of his art in the spirit of a despot of the Middle Ages throwing largesse to the mob. Except for invalids, it is fairly safe to say that when this type of artist is considered great he exists only in second-rate novels: when he exists in real life he is himself second-rate.

We who are teachers should hold up our heads more proudly. We are among the lucky ones of the earth.

If we are real artists in teaching we have the greatest joy this world can give—that of creative work.

We have also what I have called the world's greatest honour—the companionship of honourable men and women.

CHRONOLOGY

1874 Born 21 September, at Cheltenham.

1893 *Lansdown Castle*, an operetta, produced at the Corn Exchange, Cheltenham, 8 February.
Entered the Royal College of Music as a student, May.

1895 Awarded an open scholarship for composition at the Royal College of Music.

1898 Played trombone in the Carl Rosa Opera Company and the Scottish Orchestra (until 1903).

1901 Married Isobel Harrison.

1903 Gave up the trombone and began teaching at James Allen Girls' School (until 1920).

1904 Conducted the first performance of the *Suite de Ballet*, Patron's Fund concert, Queen's Hall, 20 May.

1905 Appointed Musical Director at St. Paul's Girls' School (until 1934). Conducted the first performance of *The Mystic Trumpeter*, Patron's Fund concert, Queen's Hall, 29 June.

1907 Appointed Musical Director at Morley College (until 1924).

1910 First performance of *A Somerset Rhapsody*, Edward Mason concert, Queen's Hall, April.

1912 First performance of the first group of *Choral Hymns from the Rig Veda*, Edward Mason concert, Queen's Hall, 25 March.
First performance of *Beni Mora*, Balfour Gardiner concert, Queen's Hall, 1 May.

1913 First performance of *The Cloud Messenger*, Balfour Gardiner concert, Queen's Hall, 4 March.

1916 First Whitsun festival at Thaxted, 10–12 June.
First performance of *Savitri* at the London School of Opera, conductor Hermann Grunebaum, 5 December.

1918 Private performance of *The Planets*, conductor Adrian Boult, 29 September.
Appointed Musical Organizer in the Educational Department of the Y.M.C.A. in the Middle East (until June 1919).

1919 First public performance of *The Planets*, Royal Philharmonic Society, Queen's Hall, conductor Adrian Boult, 27 February.
Appointed professor at the Royal College of Music (until 1924) and at Reading University (until 1923).

1920 First performance of *The Hymn of Jesus*, Royal Philharmonic Society, Queen's Hall, 25 March.

1923 Accident and concussion, February.
First performance of *The Perfect Fool*, British National Opera Company, Covent Garden, conductor Eugène Goossens, 14 May.
First London performance of the *Ode to Death*, Bach Choir concert, Queen's Hall, conductor Ralph Vaughan Williams, 19 December.

1924 Nervous break-down. A year's rest.

1925 First performance of *At the Boar's Head*, British National Opera Company, Manchester Opera House, conductor Malcolm Sargent, 3 April.

First London performance of the *Choral Symphony*, Royal Philharmonic Society, Queen's Hall, conductor Albert Coates, 29 October.

1927 Holst Festival at Cheltenham, 22 March.

1928 First London performance of *Egdon Heath*, Royal Philharmonic Society, Queen's Hall, conductor Vaclav Talich, 23 February.

1932 Appointed lecturer in composition at Harvard University, for six months. Taken ill in March.

1934 Operation in London on 23 May, after having been an invalid for two years.

Died 25 May.

LIST OF COMPOSITIONS

Ar.:	Edward Arnold		F.:	Faber Music
Au.:	Augener		L.:	Laudy (now Bosworth)
B. & F.:	Bayley & Ferguson		N.:	Novello
B. & H.:	Boosey & Hawkes		O.U.P.:	Oxford University Press
C.	Curwen		R.S.:	R. Smith
Cha.:	Chappell		S. & B.:	Stainer and Bell
Ches.:	Chester		Y.B.P.:	Year Book Press.
E.:	Enoch			

Manuscripts marked * are in the British Museum, Add. MSS. 47804–38.

Date	Opus	Title	Publisher
1895	1	The Revoke. Opera in one act.	MS. *
1896	2	Fantasiestücke, for oboe and strings.	MS.
	3	Quintet for piano and wind.	MS.
1896–8	4	Four Songs:	
		Margaret's Slumber Song.	L.
		Soft, soft wind.	L.
		Soft and gently.	MS.
		Awake, my heart.	MS.
	—	Light leaves whisper. Part-Song.	L.
1897	5	Clear and Cool, for five-part chorus and orchestra.	MS. *
	—	Winter Idyll, for orchestra.	MS. *
1898	6	Ornulf's Drapa, Scena for baritone and orchestra.	MS. *
		The Idea. Operetta for children.	N.
	—	Clouds o'er the summer sky. Canon.	N.
1899	7	Walt Whitman Overture.	MS. *
1900	8	Cotswolds Symphony.	MS.
1899–1900	9A	Part-Songs:	
		Love is enough.	N.
		Sylvia.	N.
		Autumn.	MS.
		Come away, death.	MS.
		Love Song.	L.
	9B	Ave Maria, for unaccompanied female voices in eight parts.	L.
	10	Suite de Ballet in E♭, for orchestra.	N.
1901–2	11	The Youth's Choice. Opera.	MS. *
1902–3	12	Part-Songs:	
		Dream Tryst.	N.
		Ye little birds.	N.
		Her eyes the glow-worm lend thee.	MS.
		Now is the month.	N.
1903	13	Indra. Symphonic poem.	MS. *
	14	Quintet for Wind.	MS.
1902–3	15	Six Baritone Songs:	
		Invocation to Dawn.	MS.
		Fain would I.	MS.
		Sergeant's Song.	E.
		In a wood.	MS.
		Between us now.	MS.
		I will not let thee go.	MS.

Date	Opus	Title	Publisher
1902–3	16	Six Soprano Songs:	
		Calm is the morn.	MS.
		My true love.	MS.
		Weep you no more.	S. & B.
		Lovely, kind.	Cha.
		Cradle song.	MS.
		Peace.	MS.
1903	—	Thou did'st delight mine eyes. Part-Song.	N.
	17	King Estmere. Ballad for chorus and orchestra.	N.
1904	18	The Mystic Trumpeter, for soprano and orchestra.	MS. *
1905	19 No. I	Song of the Night, for violin and orchestra.	MS. *
	20A	Songs from The Princess, for un-accompanied female voices:	N.
		Sweet and low.	
		The splendour falls.	
		Tears, idle tears.	
		O Swallow, Swallow.	
		Home they brought her warrior dead.	
		Now sleeps the crimson petal.	
1906	21A	Songs of the West, for orchestra.	MS. *
1906–7	21B	A Somerset Rhapsody, for orchestra.	B. & H.
1906	22	Two Songs without Words, for small orchestra:	N.
		Country Song.	
		Marching Song.	
1899–1906	23	Sita. Opera in three acts.	MS. *
1907		Song: The Heart Worships.	S. & B.
	—	Seven Scottish Airs, for strings and piano.	N.
	20B	Four Old English Carols, for chorus with piano accompaniment (also arranged for female voices):	B. & F.
		A babe is born.	
		Now let us sing.	
		Jesu, Thou the Virgin-born.	
		The Saviour of the world.	
1907–8	24	Hymns from the Rig Veda, for solo voice and piano:	Ches.
		Ushas (Dawn).	
		Varuna I (Sky).	
		Maruts (Stormclouds).	
		Indra (God of Storm).	
		Varuna II (The Waters).	
		Song of the Frogs.	
		Vac (Speech).	
		Creation.	
		Faith.	
1908	25	Savitri. Opera di camera, in one act.	C.

Date	Opus	Title	Publisher
1908	26 No. I	First Group of Choral Hymns from the Rig Veda, for chorus and orchestra: Battle Hymn. To the Unknown God. Funeral Hymn.	S. & B.
1909	26 No. II	Second Group of Choral Hymns from the Rig Veda, for female voices and orchestra: To Varuna (God of the Waters). To Agni (God of Fire). Funeral Chant.	S. & B.
1909–10	26 No. III	Third Group of Choral Hymns from the Rig Veda, for female voices and harp: Hymn to the Dawn. Hymn to the Waters. Hymn to Vena (The sun rising through the mist). Hymn of the Travellers.	S. & B.
1909	27	Incidental music to a Masque for St. Paul's Girls' School.	MS.
1909	28A	First Suite in E♭ for Military Band.	B. & H.
1910	29 No. I	Beni Mora, Suite for orchestra.	C.
	—	Christmas Day, for chorus and orchestra.	N.
	—	Four Part-Songs for children, with piano accompaniment. Words by Whittier: Song of the Ship-builders. Song of the Shoemakers. Song of the Fishermen. Song of the Drovers.	N.
	—	The swallow leaves her nest. Part-Song for unaccompanied female voices.	C.
	—	Pastoral. Part-Song for unaccompanied female voices.	S. & B.
1911	19 No. II	Invocation, for cello and orchestra.	MS. *
	—	Phantastes Suite, for orchestra (withdrawn after first performance).	MS. *
	—	Autumn Song. Part-Song.	S. & B.
	—	In youth is pleasure. Part-Song.	S. & B.
	—	O England, my Country. Unison song with orchestra.	S. & B.
	28B	Second Suite in F for Military Band.	B. & H.
	—	Two Eastern Pictures, for female voices and harp or piano: Spring. Summer.	S. & B.
	31 No. I	Hecuba's Lament, for contralto solo, chorus of female voices and orchestra.	S. & B.

Date	Opus	Title	Publisher
1912	26 No. IV	Fourth Group of Choral Hymns from the Rig Veda, for male voices, string orchestra and brass: Hymn to Agni (The sacrificial fire). Hymn to Soma (The juice of a sacrificial herb). Hymn to Manas (The spirit of a dying man). Hymn to Indra (God of heaven, storm and battle).	S. & B.
1910–12	30	The Cloud Messenger. An Ode for chorus and orchestra.	S. & B.
1912	—	Two Psalms, for chorus, string orchestra, and organ (the second is also arranged for female voices): To my humble supplication Lord, who hast made us for Thine own.	Au.
1913	29 No. II	St. Paul's Suite, for string orchestra.	C.
	31 No. II	Hymn to Dionysus, for female voices and orchestra.	S. & B.
	—	The Home-coming, for unaccompanied male voices.	S. & B.
1914	—	A Dirge for Two Veterans, for male voices, brass, and drums.	C.
1914–17	32	The Planets. Suite for orchestra: Mars, the bringer of war. Venus, the bringer of peace. Mercury, the winged messenger. Jupiter, the bringer of jollity. Saturn, the bringer of old age. Uranus, the magician. Neptune, the mystic.	C.
1915	33	Japanese Suite, for orchestra	B. & H.
	—	Nunc dimittis, for eight-part unaccompanied chorus.	MS.
1916	34	This have I done for my true love, for unaccompanied chorus.	Au.
		Carols, for unaccompanied chorus: Lullay my liking. Bring us in good ale. Of one that is so fair.	C.
		Two Carols, for chorus, with accompaniment for oboe and cello: Terly terlow. A Welcome Song.	S. & B.
		Three Carols, arranged for chorus in unison, and orchestra: Christmas Song: On this day. I saw three ships. Masters in this hall.	C.

Date	Opus	Title	Publisher
1916–17	35	Four Songs, for voice and violin:	Ches.
		Jesu sweet, now will I sing.	
		My soul has nought but fire and ice.	
		I sing of a maiden.	
		My Leman is so true.	
1916	36	Six Choral Folk-Songs, unaccompanied:	C.
		I sowed the seeds of love.	
		There was a tree.	
		Matthew, Mark.	
		The Song of the Blacksmith.	
		I love my love.	
		Swansea Town.	
		(All these songs except the second are also arranged for male voices.)	
	—	Phantasy String Quartet (withdrawn from list of compositions).	MS.
	—	Three Festival Choruses, with orchestra:	S. & B.
		Let all mortal flesh keep silence.	
		Turn back, O Man.	
		A Festival Chime.	
1917	—	Two Part-Songs for children, with piano accompaniment:	Ar.
		The Corn Song.	
		Song of the lumberman.	
	—	A Dream of Christmas, for female voices and strings or piano.	C.
	37	The Hymn of Jesus, for two choruses, semi-chorus of female voices and orchestra.	S. & B.
1919	38	Ode to Death, for chorus and orchestra.	N.
	—	Festival Te Deum, for chorus and orchestra.	S. & B.
1918–19	—	The Sneezing Charm. Ballet music for orchestra. (Later revised and used in The Perfect Fool.)	MS. *
1920	—	Seven Choruses from Alcestis, for female voices in unison, with accompaniment for harp and three flutes.	Au.
1921	—	I vow to thee, my country. Unison song with orchestral accompaniment.	C.
1918–22	39	The Perfect Fool. Opera in one act.	N.
1921–2	—	The Lure. A ballet (withdrawn from list of compositions).	MS. *
1922	40 No. I	Fugal Overture, for orchestra.	N.
1923	40 No. II	Fugal Concerto, for flute, oboe, and string orchestra.	N.
1923–4	41	First Choral Symphony, for soprano solo, chorus, and orchestra.	N.

Date	Opus	Title	Publisher
1924	42	At the Boar's Head. Opera in one act.	N.
	—	Toccata for piano, founded on a Northumbrian tune.	C.
1925	—	Terzetto, for flute, oboe, and viola.	Ches.
	43	Two motets for unaccompanied chorus:	
		The Evening Watch.	F.
		Sing me the men.	C.
1925–6	44	Seven Part-Songs. Words by Robert Bridges. For female voices and strings:	N.
		Say who is this?	
		O Love, I complain.	
		Angel spirits of sleep.	
		When first we met (A Round).	
		Sorrow and Joy.	
		Love on my heart from heaven fell.	
		Assemble all ye maidens (An Elegy).	
1926	45 No. I	The Golden Goose. A Choral Ballet.	O.U.P.
1926–7	45 No. II	The Morning of the Year. A Choral Ballet.	O.U.P.
1926	46 No. I	Chrissemas Day in the Morning, for piano.	O.U.P.
1927	46 No. II	Two Folk-Song Fragments for piano:	O.U.P.
		O I hae seen the roses blaw.	
		The Shoemakker.	
	—	Man born to toil. Anthem for chorus with organ accompaniment.	C.
	—	Eternal Father. Short anthem for soprano solo, chorus, and organ (with bells ad lib.)	C.
1927	—	The Coming of Christ. Music to a Mystery Play. For chorus, piano, organ (or string orchestra), and trumpet.	C.
1927	47	Egdon Heath. For Orchestra.	N.
1928	—	Moorside Suite for Brass Band.	R.S.
1929	48	Twelve Songs. Words by Humbert Wolfe. For solo voice and piano:	Au.
		A little music.	
		Betelgeuse.	
		Envoi.	
		In the street of lost time.	
		The Thought.	
		Things lovelier.	
		Journey's end.	
		Now in these fairylands.	
		Persephone.	
		Rhyme.	
		The Dream City.	
		The Floral Bandit.	

Date	Opus	Title	Publisher
1929	49	Double Concerto, for two violins and orchestra.	C.
1929–30	50	The Tale of the Wandering Scholar. (The Wandering Scholar) Opera	F.
1930	51	Choral Fantasia, for soprano solo, chorus, organ, strings, brass and percussion.	C.
	52	Hammersmith. A Prelude and Scherzo for orchestra. (Also for military band.)	B. & H.
	—	Nocturne, for piano.	F.
1930–1	—	Twelve Welsh Folk-Songs, arranged for unaccompanied chorus:	C.

    Lisa Lan.
    Green Grass
    The Dove.
    Awake, awake.
    Nightingale and Linnet.
    The Mother-in-law.
    The First Love.
    Monday Morning.
    My Sweetheart's like Venus.
    White Summer Rose.
    The Lively Pair.
    The Lover's Complaint.

Date	Opus	Title	Publisher
1931	—	Wassail Song, arranged for unaccompanied chorus.	C.
	—	Roadways. Unison Song.	Y.B.P.
1931–2	—	Six Choruses for male voices, with accompaniment for strings, organ or piano. Words translated by Helen Waddell:	B. & H.

    Intercession.
    Good Friday.
    Drinking Song.
    Love Song.
    How mighty are the Sabbaths.
    (Also in a unison setting.)
    Before Sleep.

Date	Opus	Title	Publisher
1932	—	Six Canons for equal voices, unaccompanied. Words translated by Helen Waddell.	F.

    For three voices:
     If you love songs.
     Lovely Venus.
     The fields of sorrow.
     David's Lament for Jonathan.
    For three choirs (nine voices):
     O strong of heart.
    For two choirs (six voices):
     Truth of all truth.

Date	Opus	Title	Publisher
1932	—	Two Canons, for equal voices and piano: Evening on the Moselle. If 'twere the time of lilies.	F.
	—	Jig, for piano.	F.
	—	Capriccio for orchestra (originally 'Jazz band piece').	F.
1933	—	Brook Green Suite, for string orchestra (with ad lib. wood-wind parts).	C.
	—	Lyric Movement, for viola and small orchestra.	O.U.P.
1933–4	—	Scherzo, for orchestra (from an unfinished symphony).	B. & H.

Works edited by Holst include the Festival Chorus, All people that on earth do dwell (S. & B.), Sacred Rounds and Canons, and Old Airs and Glees, for equal voices (S. & B.), and Suites for String Orchestra by Purcell, with additional ad lib. wind and timpani parts (N.).

INDEX

(Figures in bold type indicate the main reference to a work)